Bible Stories and Trivia for Teens

Grow Strong in Faith with Christian Lessons, Biblical Truths, Prayers, and 600 Fun Quiz Questions

Welcome Aboard, Check Out This Limited-Time Free Bonus!

Ahoy, reader! Welcome to the Ahoy Publications family, and thanks for snagging a copy of this book! Since you've chosen to join us on this journey, we'd like to offer you something special.

Check out the link below for a FREE e-book filled with delightful facts about American History.

But that's not all - you'll also have access to our exclusive email list with even more free e-books and insider knowledge. Well, what are ye waiting for? Click the link below to join and set sail toward exciting adventures in American History.

Access your bonus here
https://ahoypublications.com/
Or, Scan the QR code!

Table of Contents

PART 1: BIBLE STORIES FOR TEENS 1

INTRODUCTION 3

SECTION 1: FINDING YOUR IDENTITY IN GOD (GENESIS -
EXODUS) 5

    CHAPTER 1: CREATION — MADE FOR A REASON.............................7

    CHAPTER 2: ENOCH WALKS WITH GOD — A QUIET LIFE
    THAT PLEASED GOD 10

    CHAPTER 3: NOAH — TRUST IN THE STORM 13

    CHAPTER 4: ABRAHAM — FOLLOWING WHEN YOU'RE
    AFRAID...15

    CHAPTER 5: JACOB WRESTLES WITH GOD — BECOMING
    WHO YOU'RE MEANT TO BE 17

    CHAPTER 6: JOSEPH — TRUSTING GOD'S PLAN THROUGH
    PAIN...19

    CHAPTER 7: JOSEPH FORGIVES HIS BROTHERS —
    FORGIVENESS OVER REVENGE...22

    CHAPTER 8: MOSES — YOUR VOICE MATTERS TO GOD 24

SECTION 2: COURAGE WHEN LIFE GETS TOUGH (JOSHUA -
ESTHER) 27

    CHAPTER 9: JOSHUA — BRAVE STEPS FORWARD 29

    CHAPTER 10: DEBORAH — LEADING WITH COURAGE.................32

    CHAPTER 11: GIDEON — GOD'S STRENGTH IN YOUR
    WEAKNESS 35

    CHAPTER 12: RUTH — LOYALTY THAT CHANGES
    EVERYTHING 37

    CHAPTER 13: SAMUEL'S CALLING — HEARING GOD'S
    VOICE...40

    CHAPTER 14: DAVID AND GOLIATH — BE STRONG, EVEN
    WHEN YOU'RE SMALL...43

    CHAPTER 15: ELIJAH RUNS AND HEARS GOD — GOD
    SPEAKS IN THE QUIET 46

CHAPTER 16: KING HEZEKIAH – PRAYING WHEN EVERYTHING FALLS APART 49

CHAPTER 17: SHADRACH, MESHACH, AND ABEDNEGO – FAITH IN THE FIRE 52

CHAPTER 18: DANIEL IN THE LION'S DEN – TRUST WHEN YOU'RE SURROUNDED 55

CHAPTER 19: ESTHER – YOU WERE BORN FOR THIS MOMENT 58

SECTION 3: RETURNING TO GOD – MERCY AND SECOND CHANCES (JOB - JONAH) 61

CHAPTER 20: JOB – FAITH IN THE MIDDLE OF PAIN 63

CHAPTER 21: NEHEMIAH – BUILDING DREAMS WITH GOD'S HELP 66

CHAPTER 22: JONAH – RUNNING FROM GOD'S CALL 69

SECTION 4: ENCOUNTERING JESUS – LOVE THAT TRANSFORMS (MATTHEW-JOHN) 73

CHAPTER 23: BIRTH OF JESUS – HOPE IN THE HARD TIMES 75

CHAPTER 24: THE WOMAN WHO TOUCHED JESUS'S ROBE – FAITH THAT REACHES OUT 78

CHAPTER 25: JESUS FEEDS THE 5,000 – TRUSTING GOD WITH WHAT YOU HAVE 81

CHAPTER 26: PETER WALKS ON WATER – KEEPING YOUR EYES ON JESUS 83

CHAPTER 27: JESUS CALMS THE STORM – FINDING PEACE INSIDE CHAOS 86

CHAPTER 28: JESUS AND THE WOMAN AT THE WELL – FULLY KNOWN AND LOVED 89

CHAPTER 29: THE GOOD SAMARITAN – LOVING PEOPLE WHO ARE DIFFERENT 92

CHAPTER 30: MARY AND MARTHA – CHOOSING WHAT MATTERS MOST 95

CHAPTER 31: JESUS AND THE ADULTEROUS WOMAN – GRACE INSTEAD OF SHAME 98

CHAPTER 32: ZACCHAEUS – SEEN AND CHANGED BY LOVE 101

CHAPTER 33: THE LOST SON – ALWAYS WELCOME HOME 104

CHAPTER 34: JESUS WASHES THE DISCIPLES' FEET – SERVING WITH LOVE 107

CHAPTER 35: CRUCIFIXION AND RESURRECTION – STRONGER THAN DEATH.....................................110

CHAPTER 36: THE THIEF ON THE CROSS – IT'S NEVER TOO LATE..................................113

CHAPTER 37: THOMAS DOUBTS – WHEN YOU NEED PROOF..................................116

CHAPTER 38: PETER IS RESTORED – WHEN YOU'VE MESSED UP BIG..................................119

SECTION 5: FAITH THAT CHANGES THE WORLD (ACTS - REVELATION)..................................123

CHAPTER 39: STEPHEN STANDS STRONG – FAITH THAT SPEAKS BOLDLY..................................125

CHAPTER 40: PENTECOST – THE POWER TO CHANGE THE WORLD..................................128

CHAPTER 41: PAUL'S STORY – GOD CAN USE ANYONE.............131

CHAPTER 42: PHILIP AND THE ETHIOPIAN – SHARING YOUR FAITH NATURALLY..................................134

CHAPTER 43: ARMOR OF GOD – PROTECTION FOR TOUGH DAYS..................................137

CHAPTER 44: NEW HEAVEN AND NEW EARTH – HOPE THAT NEVER DIES..................................140

CLOSING WORDS: YOUR JOURNEY IS JUST BEGINNING.................142

GOING DEEPER – OPTIONAL STUDY TRACK..................................144

CHARACTER PROFILES – REAL PEOPLE, REAL FAITH..................149

KEY CONCEPTS EXPLAINED – FOUNDATIONS OF YOUR FAITH..................................154

MEMORY VERSE CHALLENGES – HIDE GOD'S WORD IN YOUR HEART..................................158

PART 2: THE ULTIMATE BIBLE TRIVIA BOOK FOR TEENS..................161

SECTION 1: GENESIS - REVELATION..................................163

SUBSECTION 1: THE BEGINNING: WAY BACK WHEN IT ALL STARTED..................................165

SUBSECTION 2: NOAH'S EPIC VOYAGE & THE TOWER THAT TRIED TOO HARD!..................................171

SUBSECTION 3: FROM ONE FAMILY TO A NATION..................176

SUBSECTION 4: FROM SLAVERY TO EXODUS - LET MY PEOPLE GO!..................................181

SUBSECTION 5: WILDERNESS WANDERINGS & THE PROMISED LAND - THE ULTIMATE ROAD TRIP (WITH DETOURS!)..................................186

SUBSECTION 6: KINGS, PROPHETS, AND EXILE - THE UPS AND DOWNS OF A NATION 191

SUBSECTION 7: JESUS AND THE GOSPELS - THE MAIN EVENT BEGINS!.. 196

SUBSECTION 8: THE EARLY CHURCH AND REVELATION - THE STORY CONTINUES 201

SECTION 2: AWESOME PEOPLE OF THE BIBLE 207

SUBSECTION 1: THE FAITH HALL OF FAMERS (OLD TESTAMENT HEROES) 209

SUBSECTION 2: JESUS' INNER CIRCLE - THE TWELVE DISCIPLES... 214

SUBSECTION 3: GAME CHANGERS - OTHER INFLUENTIAL PEOPLE 219

SUBSECTION 4: TRICKY TALES - COMPLEX OR CONTROVERSIAL FIGURES 224

SECTION 3: THEME PARK - EXPLORING KEY BIBLICAL THEMES.. 229

SUBSECTION 1: LOVE & RELATIONSHIPS (GOD'S LOVE, FRIENDSHIP, FAMILY)... 231

SUBSECTION 2: FORGIVENESS & REDEMPTION (SECOND CHANCES, GRACE) 236

SUBSECTION 3: FAITH & TRUST (BELIEVING IN GOD, EVEN WHEN IT'S HARD)... 241

SUBSECTION 4: HOPE & PERSEVERANCE 246

SUBSECTION 5: PRAYER & WORSHIP 251

SUBSECTION 6: WISDOM & GUIDANCE.................................... 256

SUBSECTION 7: JUSTICE & MERCY 261

SUBSECTION 8: COURAGE & RISK-TAKING............................. 266

SECTION 4 – LIGHTNING ROUND (100 RAPID-FIRE QUESTIONS) (ALL MULTIPLE-CHOICE; KEEP THEM QUICK!) 271

SECTION 5 – ULTIMATE CHALLENGE 291

EXTRA ROUND: WOMEN OF THE WORD (50 QUESTIONS) 301

WELCOME ABOARD, CHECK OUT THIS LIMITED-TIME FREE BONUS!... 316

CHECK OUT ANOTHER BOOK IN THE SERIES 317

WELCOME ABOARD, CHECK OUT THIS LIMITED-TIME FREE BONUS!... 318

Part 1: Bible Stories for Teens

Christian Lessons, Biblical Truths, and Prayers to Help Teenagers Grow Strong in Faith

Introduction

If you're holding this book in your hands, I want you to know something really important right from the start: It has been written for teen readers just like you!

Maybe you've tried reading the Bible before and didn't know where to start, or wondered: What is the most important thing I need to learn from a story I have just read?

As the author of this book, I want you to know: I get it. Sometimes, we grow up with adults or other authority figures telling us what to believe, but without any context – it's like learning a science formula but without the why or how.

Yet, the Bible is a Holy Book filled with incredible stories divinely inspired to provide us with guidance for everyday life. Stories of creation and how it still relates to us today, scripture of how people persevered during tough times, and how, even when things look bleak.

The selection of Bible stories that you are about to read have been lovingly curated to help you in your journey of growing in faith and growing closer to God. It includes true life recollections of everyday people. Those that doubted, messed up, ran from God, felt afraid, got rejected, had anxiety, and faced temptation.

But, as you will see in this collection of quick-read stories, God never gave up on them. Just like He will never give up on us. So, get ready to revisit incredible stories, what they mean for us today, and how they connect to modern life.

Get ready for bonus content too!

Inside this book, I've included:

- **Short, powerful lessons** that fit into your schedule.
- **Real prayers** you can say out loud or in your heart.
- **Big questions** to help you think about what you believe.
- **Truth** you can stand on when life gets messy.

Be sure to read until the end, as there is a bonus study track for when you would like to go deeper into the history of Bible stories and heroes.

Get ready to discover and learn incredible Bible truths in every story. Enjoy this beautiful volume, may you treasure it for years to come!

Section 1: Finding Your Identity in God (Genesis – Exodus)

Who are you really?

That's a question a lot of us ask, especially when life feels confusing or when we're trying to figure out who we're supposed to be. The truth is, the Bible starts by answering that very question!

In this section, you'll meet the first people God created, and others who were far from perfect. Yet, they were still deeply loved and chosen by Him. You'll read about Adam, Enoch, Noah, Abraham, Jacob, Joseph, and Moses. Each of their stories is different, but they all show us something important: Your true identity isn't found in what others say, what you've done, or even how you feel about yourself. Your identity is found in your Heavenly Creator who made you, sees you, and calls you by name.

Whether you're strong like Noah, afraid like Abraham, struggling like Jacob, or unsure like Moses, God has a purpose for you.

Chapter 1: Creation — Made for a Reason

The Bible Story (Genesis 1-2, Retold)

In the very beginning, there was nothing but darkness and emptiness.

Then God spoke. He said, "Let there be light," and **boom!** — there was light.

He made the oceans and the mountains, the trees and the flowers, the birds in the sky and the fish in the sea.

God did not create people with a word. He formed the man from dust and gave him breath (Genesis 2:7). He built the woman from the man's side (Genesis 2:22). This was not casual. It was direct and intentional.

God called the whole creation "very good" only after it was finished (Genesis 1:31). That statement was about the completed order, not about Adam and Eve alone.

Humans were made in the image of God (Genesis 1:27). That means they were created to reflect His authority, reason, and purpose. It means bearing weight, not chasing worth.

You were made to reflect God, not to impress the world. Your purpose is not to feel special. Your purpose is to live under His design. That is enough.

Takeaway: You Were Created For A Special Purpose

Sometimes the world can make you feel like you have to prove yourself. You might think:

"If I could just be more popular...

If I could just get better grades...

If I could just fit in... then maybe I'd matter."

But the truth is, you are in the right place at the right time because of **Who** made you.

God created you on purpose, with a purpose. You were created by the same God who painted the skies and carved out oceans. He sees the potential in you, even when you don't. You are **called, seen and loved.** And you are made to live a life that reflects His love and light in ways only you can.

Reflection Questions

- When have you felt like you didn't matter, or like you had to earn your worth?

- What do you call 'very good' in your life? Is it a thing? A Person? How do you treat the things you call very good?

- If you are created on purpose, for a purpose, what might that mean for how you live today?

(Write your thoughts below, share them with someone you trust, or simply take a few quiet moments to reflect.)

_____

_____

_____

_____

_____

_____

Prayer

God,

Thank You for making me on purpose.

When I feel small or invisible, remind me that You see me.

Help me believe that I am Your masterpiece.

Show me the plans You have for my life.

I want to walk with You every day.

Amen.

Faith Challenge

Today, whenever you look in the mirror, say this out loud:

"I am made by God. I am very good."

Say it even if you don't feel it yet.

Say it until your heart starts to believe it.

You were made for a reason. Never forget it.

Chapter 2: Enoch Walks with God — A Quiet Life That Pleased God

The Bible tells us about a man named Enoch, someone who stood out in a way the world often misses: He simply walked with God.

Let's take a look at his story.

The Bible Story (Genesis 5:21-24, Retold)

Enoch lived in the early generations after creation. Like the others in his line, he lived many years, but with one clear difference.

Scripture says, "Enoch walked with God" (Genesis 5:22). And then, "he was not, for God took him" (Genesis 5:24). There is no mention of death.

Hebrews 11:5 explains it further: "By faith Enoch was taken up so that he should not see death, and he was not found, because God had taken him." His removal was not ordinary. It was an exception, made by God, recorded without detail, and never repeated in the same way.

What set Enoch apart was not his age, but his walk. He lived in step with God, faithfully. That is what the record tells us.

Enoch left no speech, no monument, no kingdom. But his faith was remembered. Thousands of years later, his name still stands for one thing: obedience.

Takeaway: You Don't Have to Be Loud to Live Meaningfully

Enoch's story is proof that you just need to **walk with God** with steady trust, quiet faith, and a heart that stays close to Him. In today's world, it's easy to think that louder is better, that influence only comes from platforms, followers, or applause.

But God sees something deeper. He sees your small, daily choices. He sees your faith when no one else is watching. He hears your whispered prayers. He notices when you choose kindness over attention, obedience over popularity, and truth over trends.

God treasures the faithful and uses the simple, humble lives of people like Enoch, and you, to show the world what real faith looks like.

Reflection Questions

- What do you think faithfulness in God looks like today?
- What's one small, quiet habit, such as prayer, gratitude, or reading Scripture, that could help you stay close to Him this week?

(Write or reflect in your own way. God speaks even in stillness.)

_____

_____

_____

_____

_____

_____

_____

Prayer

God,

Sometimes I feel like I'm not doing enough.

But Enoch's story reminds me that just walking with You is powerful.

Help me trust that my quiet faith matters.

Help me stay close to You, even when no one's watching.

I want to walk with You every day.

Amen.

Faith Challenge

Today, take a 10-minute walk, just you and God.

Leave your phone behind.

As you walk, pray quietly.

You don't need fancy words.

Just talk to God like a friend.

And then listen.

Sometimes, the most powerful steps are the quiet ones.

Chapter 3: Noah — Trust in the Storm

Have you ever felt like you're the only one standing up for something right? Like everyone around you is doing one thing, but deep down, you know it's not right? It's hard to be the only one.

But there's a story about a man who stood alone and trusted God through the biggest storm the world had ever seen. Let's read more about Noah.

The Bible Story (Genesis 6–9, Retold)

The Bible says that generations after Adam and Eve, the world became corrupt. Cain murdered his brother. Violence spread. People ignored God and followed their own desires.

"Every intention of the thoughts of man's heart was only evil continually" (Genesis 6:5). God saw it. And He judged it.

The Lord said, "I will blot out man whom I have created from the face of the land" (Genesis 6:7). The flood was not a reset. It was judgment.

But one man found favor.

Noah walked with God (Genesis 6:9). While the rest of the world ignored truth, Noah listened. God gave him a command: build an ark. A flood was coming, and only those inside would be saved.

God told Noah to bring two of every unclean animal and seven pairs of every clean animal, and birds too (Genesis 7:2-3). This wasn't a myth. It was a command with structure and purpose.

Noah obeyed. He built the ark. He prepared. And when the waters came, everything outside was destroyed. Only Noah, his family, and those with him in the ark survived.

After the flood, God established a covenant. He set a rainbow in the sky as a sign of His promise: never again would He destroy the earth with a flood (Genesis 9:13-15).

God did what He said. He always does.

Takeaway: Trust Even When It Doesn't Make Sense

Sometimes doing the right thing feels lonely, and trusting God might feel risky. But remember this: God sees everything. He has a plan even when you don't understand it yet.

When you stand alone for what's right, you're never alone. God is standing with you, and when the storm hits, He is always your shelter.

Trust Him. Even when it's hard. Even when it's scary or it feels like no one else gets it. Because God always keeps His promises.

Reflection Questions

- When have you felt like the only one standing for something right?
- What aspects of God in Noah's story makes him trustworthy?

Prayer

God,

Help me trust You, even when it's hard.

Give me courage when I feel alone.

Remind me that You are with me, even when no one else is.

Build my faith like You built the ark: Strong enough to handle any storm.

Amen.

Faith Challenge

Pick one small thing today where you can trust God more.

It could be choosing kindness when others aren't, being honest, even if it's hard, or praying about something scary instead of worrying.

Whatever it is, take that one step. Trust Him with it. You're building something stronger than an ark: A life of faith.

Chapter 4: Abraham — Following When You're Afraid

Have you ever had to step into something completely new without knowing how it would turn out, such as a new school or trying out for a sports team?

It's scary to take a step when you can't see the whole road ahead, but that's exactly the kind of faith God calls us to. That's what Abraham had to learn.

The Bible Story (Genesis 12–21, Retold)

Abram lived in the city of Ur. He had land, family, and a stable life. Then God gave him a command: leave your country, your relatives, and your father's house, and go to the land that I will show you (Genesis 12:1). God promised to make Abram into a great nation, to bless him, and to make his name great so that he would be a blessing (Genesis 12:2).

Abram obeyed. He left everything and followed. As he traveled, God spoke again. But Abram and his wife Sarai remained childless. The promise stood, but the evidence did not appear. Then God brought Abram outside and said, "Look toward heaven, and number the stars, if you are able to number them. So shall your offspring be" (Genesis 15:5).

God made a covenant with Abram. He believed the Lord, and it was counted to him as righteousness (Genesis 15:6).

Time passed. God did not forget. He changed Abram's name to Abraham, meaning "father of many" (Genesis 17:5). He also changed Sarai's name to Sarah (Genesis 17:15).

Then the Lord did what He had said. Sarah gave birth to a son, Isaac (Genesis 21:1-3). Not because they understood. Not because they were strong. But because God always keeps His word.

Abraham's story is about trust. Trust when the outcome is not visible. Trust when nothing makes sense. Faith is not theory. It is action.

Takeaway: Faith Is Following Before You See

Faith is not about knowing the outcome. It is about trusting the One who commands. When God called Abraham, He did not reveal the full plan. He gave a command, and Abraham obeyed (Genesis 12:1-4).

God does not ask for achievement. He requires trust. Obedience matters more than understanding. Faith walks forward even when the path is unclear.

Reflection Questions

- How has this story helped you to better understand what it means to trust God?
- What's one area of your life where God might be asking you to trust Him more today?

Prayer

God,

Sometimes I'm scared to take steps when I can't see where they lead.

Help me trust You like Abraham did.

Help me follow even when it feels uncertain.

I believe You have good plans for me.

Give me courage to walk by faith, not just by sight.

Amen.

Faith Challenge

Think of one area where you're feeling unsure or afraid right now, such as a decision or a change you need to make. Pray about it, asking God to lead you step-by-step. Then, move forward in faith today. Trust that God is already ahead of you, making a way.

Chapter 5: Jacob Wrestles with God — Becoming Who You're Meant to Be

Have you ever felt stuck between who you are and who you want to be? Have you made mistakes you're not proud of, or are you scared of what lies ahead?

It sounds like you have a lot in common with Jacob. He was caught between a messy past and an unknown future. Luckily, in the middle of the night, something surprising happened that would change Jacob's future.

Jacob wrestled with God, and in that moment of struggle, everything changed.

The Bible Story (Genesis 32:22–31, Retold)

Jacob was going home. He was also going to face Esau, the brother he had deceived. Years earlier, Jacob had taken both the birthright and the blessing that belonged to Esau. He had lived by grasping, bargaining, and fleeing.

Now Esau was approaching with four hundred men. Jacob feared the worst. He sent his family across the river and stayed behind alone.

That night, a man came and wrestled with him until daybreak. They struggled without rest. When the man said, "Let me go," Jacob answered, "I will not let you go unless you bless me" (Genesis 32:26).

The man asked his name. Jacob answered. Then the man said, "Your name shall no longer be called Jacob, but Israel, for you have striven with God and with men, and have prevailed" (Genesis 32:28).

Jacob understood that he had encountered more than a man. He had wrestled with God. He limped away with a new name, a changed posture, and a memory of struggle.

The covenant had already been spoken at Bethel (Genesis 28). This was not a new promise. It was a turning point. Not a blessing earned, but an identity given.

Takeaway: God Meets You in the Struggle

Sometimes, we think we need to be perfect for God to bless us. But Jacob's story says the opposite. God met Jacob in the middle of fear, guilt, and struggle, and that's where God often meets us too.

God didn't reject Jacob. He renamed him, and He can do the same for you.

Reflection Questions

- What are you wrestling with right now? Is it fear, guilt, pressure, confusion?

- How might God be using your struggle to help you grow?

- What name would you want God to speak over your life? Brave, forgiven, chosen?

Prayer

God,

Sometimes I feel stuck.

I wrestle with fear, regret, and doubt.

But I believe You meet me in the struggle.

Change my heart.

Help me become who You made me to be.

Amen.

Faith Challenge

Write down one thing you're wrestling with, then bring it to God in prayer.

Say this out loud: "God, I won't let go until You bless me."

Trust that He hears you and that on the other side of the struggle is something new.

Chapter 6: Joseph — Trusting God's Plan Through Pain

Have you ever had a time when everything seemed to fall apart? Perhaps you had an argument with your best friend, or someone blamed you for something that wasn't your fault at all.

Maybe your dreams felt crushed, and you wondered, *"Where is God in all of this?"* Pain can make it feel like God has left you, but so often, the hardest moments are where His biggest plans begin. No one knew that better than Joseph.

The Bible Story (Genesis 37–50, Retold)

Joseph grew up in a big family with eleven brothers, and he was clearly his father's favorite. His dad even gave him a special colorful coat to show it.

Naturally, his brothers were jealous. One day, they'd had enough. They threw Joseph into a pit and sold him to slave traders. They took Joseph's robe, tore it, and dipped it in animal blood. When they brought it back to their father, he believed Joseph had been killed by a wild animal.

Meanwhile, Joseph was taken far away to Egypt. Yet, even there, God was with him. He worked hard as a servant in the house of a powerful man named Potiphar and earned his trust. But just when things seemed to be turning around, Potiphar's wife told a terrible lie. She accused Joseph of trying to hurt her, even though he had done nothing wrong. Joseph was thrown into prison for a crime he didn't commit.

Still, Joseph didn't give up. He kept trusting God. He interpreted dreams for two of Pharaoh's officials: The king's cupbearer and baker who had been thrown into jail. He explained exactly what their dreams meant, and just as he said, one of them was released and restored to his job.

When Pharaoh himself had disturbing dreams that no one could explain, the cupbearer remembered Joseph. Joseph was brought from prison to the palace. With God's help, he interpreted Pharaoh's dreams, warning of seven years of plenty followed by seven years of famine.

Pharaoh was so amazed, he made Joseph second-in-command over all of Egypt. Then, when the famine hit, people came from all over looking for food, including Joseph's brothers. They didn't recognize him at first. But instead of getting revenge, Joseph forgave them. He helped them and saved his whole family.

Joseph's pain wasn't the end of the story. It was part of God's bigger plan.

Takeaway: Pain Doesn't Cancel God's Purpose

It's easy to believe that God is good when life feels good. But what about when nothing makes sense? Joseph's story reminds us that pain doesn't mean God has disappeared.

It means God is **preparing something deeper.**

Joseph was sold by his brothers, wrongly accused, thrown into prison, and forgotten for years. But none of that stopped God's plan. In fact, God used every setback to lead Joseph into his calling.

When you're in the middle of heartbreak or confusion, it's hard to see the big picture. But remember: God is still writing your story, and he's still faithful.

So, if you're in a hard season, don't give up. You may not see it now, but God is inspiring you to grow strength, wisdom, and compassion.

Reflection Questions

- When have you felt like everything was going wrong, like God was distant or silent?

- What might God be building in you through a season of waiting, heartbreak, or confusion?

- How does Joseph's story help you trust God's plan even when it's not easy to understand?

(Pause. Reflect. Write. Pray. Let God meet you in the middle of the hard parts.)

Prayer

God,

Sometimes pain feels too heavy to carry.

Help me remember that You are with me even in the hardest times.

Use the things that hurt to grow my heart stronger in faith.

Help me trust Your plan, even when I can't see it yet.

Amen.

Faith Challenge

Think about something painful you've gone through or are going through now. Write down one way God might use it for good, even if you can't see it clearly yet.

Keep that note somewhere you'll see it often as a reminder: **God can bring purpose out of your pain.**

Chapter 7: Joseph Forgives His Brothers — Forgiveness Over Revenge

Have you ever been hurt by someone you trusted such as a best friend or someone you loved? When you're hurt, the easiest thing to want is revenge.

But Joseph's story shows a different way: the power of forgiveness. Let's continue where we left off in the previous story.

The Bible Story (Genesis 45, Retold)

The moment had finally come.

Joseph stood in front of the very brothers who had betrayed him, who had tossed him in a pit and sold him as a slave. Years had passed. He had been ripped from his home, thrown into prison for a crime he didn't commit, and forgotten by almost everyone. But not by God.

Now, Joseph was second-in-command over all of Egypt. His brothers had come, unaware of who he really was, desperate for food in a time of famine. Joseph had every right to be angry, every reason to say, "You don't deserve my help."

But instead, he revealed his true identity to his brothers. Yes, they had hurt him. Yes, their choices had changed everything. But Joseph saw something bigger. He saw God's hand at work.

He hugged his brothers. He wept. He promised to take care of them and their families. He didn't erase the past, but he chose to write a new future.

Joseph could have passed the pain on. Instead, he broke the cycle.

Reflection Questions

- When have you been hurt by someone and struggled to forgive?
- What would it look like to trust God with that hurt instead of holding onto revenge?

Prayer

God,

Forgiveness is hard.

Sometimes my heart wants to hold onto anger and pain.

Help me trust You enough to forgive — not because the hurt was okay, but because Your love is greater than the hurt.

Heal my heart.

Teach me to forgive like You forgive me.

Amen.

Faith Challenge

Think of someone you are struggling to forgive. Pray for them today — even if it's just a simple prayer:

"God, help them. Bless them. Heal my heart."

Forgiveness isn't always a feeling. Sometimes, it starts with a prayer — and God does the rest.

Chapter 8: Moses — Your Voice Matters to God

Have you ever felt like you weren't good enough to do something important? Maybe you were too nervous to speak up in class, or thought someone else was smarter, cooler, or stronger.

Maybe you wanted to make a difference but felt like your voice wouldn't matter. Moses felt the same way.

But God showed him, and can show you, that when He calls you, He also gives you everything you need.

The Bible Story (Exodus 3-4, Retold)

Moses was born a Hebrew but raised in Pharaoh's house. Though he lived among royalty, he saw the oppression of his people. One day, he witnessed an Egyptian beating a Hebrew. In anger, Moses struck and killed the Egyptian (Exodus 2:11-12). When the act became known, he fled to Midian.

In Midian, Moses lived as a shepherd. He married, kept flocks, and remained far from Egypt for many years. Then, one day, while tending sheep near Horeb, he saw a bush that burned but was not consumed. He approached it. God called to him from the fire (Exodus 3:4).

God said, "I have surely seen the affliction of My people... I have come down to deliver them... Come, I will send you to Pharaoh" (Exodus 3:7-10).

Moses hesitated. He questioned his ability. He asked what he should say and how the people would believe him. God answered each concern.

He declared His name, gave signs, and promised, "I will be with you" (Exodus 3:12).

Moses was not chosen because of strength or confidence. He was chosen because God sent him. The mission was not about Moses. It was about obedience to God's command.

Takeaway: God Doesn't Call the Perfect — He Calls the Willing

You don't have to be the loudest voice in the room. You don't need to have all the right words, a polished story, or unshakable confidence.

When God called Moses, Moses didn't feel ready. He was unsure of his voice, nervous about speaking, and filled with self-doubt. He even begged God to send someone else. But God didn't give up on him.

Instead, He gave Moses exactly what he needed, including his brother Aaron to speak on his behalf (Exodus 7:1–2). Moses didn't go alone. God sent help.

God knows your fears. He knows your insecurities, and He still says, "I want to use you." Even if your voice shakes or you feel someone else could do a better job.

God isn't waiting for you to have it all together. He just wants your yes. When you trust Him, He fills in the gaps with strength, clarity, courage, and sometimes even people to walk alongside you.

You don't have to lead perfectly or speak flawlessly. You just have to trust the One who called you.

Reflection Questions

- When have you felt like you weren't bold enough, strong enough, or qualified?
- Is there a place in your life where God might be inviting you to trust Him?
- What would it look like to say, "God, I'm not perfect ... but I'm willing"?

(Take a moment. Breathe. Let your "yes" be the start of something big.)

Prayer

God,

Sometimes I feel small.

Sometimes I feel like my voice doesn't matter.

But You say it does.

Help me trust that You can use me, even when I feel weak.

Give me courage to say yes to whatever You are asking me to do.

Amen.

Faith Challenge

Today, if you feel nervous about speaking up, trying something new, or standing up for what's right. Take one brave step, even if it feels small. Trust that God is with you and that your voice matters. Every big story starts with one small yes.

Section 2: Courage When Life Gets Tough (Joshua – Esther)

What do you do when life feels too big for you? In this part of the Bible, we meet people who faced real fear, real danger, and real struggles, just like we do. They didn't always feel brave, but each one chose to trust God in the middle of it. From warriors like Joshua and Deborah, to unlikely heroes like Ruth and Esther, these stories show us that courage isn't about having all the answers, it's about trusting the One who does. The same God who gave them strength is ready to do the same for you.

Chapter 9: Joshua — Brave Steps Forward

Have you ever had a moment when you knew you had to do something scary? You knew you had to be brave, but being brave didn't mean you weren't afraid.

It meant you trusted something bigger than fear. Joshua knew that feeling, and he showed us how to take brave steps forward, even when the road looks impossible.

The Bible Story (Joshua 1–6, Retold)

Before Joshua ever stepped into leadership, God had already written a long story with His people. The Israelites had once been slaves in Egypt, but God rescued them through powerful miracles. He made a covenant with them, a promise that they would be His people, and He would be their God. He promised to bring them to a land of their own.

But after their rescue from Egypt, the people didn't trust God fully. They complained. They doubted. They disobeyed. And because of that, they wandered in the desert for forty years.

Now, that long journey was finally coming to an end.

Moses, their great leader, had passed away. God chose Joshua to take his place. Joshua had some huge shoes to fill. He wasn't just leading a group of people, he was leading a whole nation into the next chapter of God's promise. But there was still one big problem. The Promised Land wasn't empty. It was filled with strong armies, fortified cities, and enemies who weren't planning to move out.

God saw Joshua's fear and spoke clearly to him: "Be strong and courageous. Don't be afraid or discouraged. I will be with you wherever you go" (Joshua 1:9).

So Joshua chose to trust God, even when the next step didn't make much sense. The first challenge? The city of Jericho. A massive fortress with high, thick walls.

But instead of battle plans, God gave Joshua instructions that sounded more like a marching band routine. Walk around the city once a day for six days. On the seventh day, walk around it seven times, then blow your trumpets and shout.

It sounded impossible, but Joshua obeyed.

On the seventh day, when the people shouted, the walls came crashing down. Joshua won the battle thanks to making space for God's power to move.

Takeaway: God Is Faithful Even When We Struggle to Trust Him

The story of Joshua is a symbol of how God keeping His promises, even to a people who didn't always keep theirs. For generations, the Israelites had seen God provide. He rescued them from slavery and gave them food in the wilderness. Now, He was leading them into the land He had promised long ago.

God's instructions to Joshua were about trust. Would God's people believe Him enough to follow Him, even when it didn't make sense?

Joshua obeyed, because he remembered who God was: the One who had never broken a promise. That's the heart of this story.

When we feel unsure or unsteady, we can look back and remember all the ways God has come through. He's trustworthy.

Reflection Questions

- What is something in your life right now that feels scary, overwhelming, or uncertain?
- What would it look like to face that challenge **with God** instead of trying to figure it out alone?
- Is there one step you can take today that says, "God, I trust You"?

(You don't have to feel ready. You just have to be willing to move forward with Him.)

Prayer

God,

Sometimes I feel afraid when I face big challenges.

Help me remember that You are bigger than anything standing in my way.

Give me courage to take brave steps, even when the path looks scary.

Help me trust Your power, not just my own.

Amen.

Faith Challenge

Pick one challenge you are facing today.

Pray about it.

Then take one step of faith, even if it's a small one.

Maybe it's speaking up. Maybe it's choosing kindness. Maybe it's standing strong when others don't.

Your brave step opens the door for God to move.

Chapter 10: Deborah — Leading with Courage

Have you ever thought leadership was only for certain types of people? Maybe the loudest voice, the most popular person, or the strongest athlete? Maybe you've felt like leadership was for someone else, not you.

God often calls unexpected people to lead. People who are willing to listen to His voice, stand strong, and trust Him completely. Deborah's story shows that courage, not popularity, is what makes a real leader.

The Bible Story (Judges 4–5, Retold)

Long after Gideon's time, Israel faced another enemy: A cruel king named Jabin and his general, Sisera. Their army had **900 iron chariots,** which made them unbeatable in battle. The Israelites were suffering under Jabin's rule.

In the middle of this chaos, there was a woman named Deborah. She wasn't a warrior or a king. She was a prophet, someone who listened to God and shared His truth. She also served as a judge, helping people solve their problems.

One day, Deborah called for a man named Barak. She told him:

"The Lord commands you: Go, take 10,000 men and fight Sisera. God will give you victory." (Judges 4:6)

Barak was nervous. He said, *"I'll only go if you go with me."*

Deborah agreed. She wasn't afraid. Together, they led the people into battle. Just like God promised, Sisera's army was defeated, because God fought for them.

Deborah's courage and obedience helped save her people. She didn't lead by being the loudest or the strongest. She led by trusting God completely.

Takeaway: Leadership Is About Trusting God

Leadership in God's kingdom looks different. Deborah wasn't loud or pushy. She was **wise**, **faithful**, and **courageous**.

She listened to God, trusted His voice, and acted when others froze in fear. That's what made her a leader: Her trust.

If God is calling you to lead, even in a small way, that's enough. He doesn't expect you to lead in your own strength. He promises to go before you, beside you, and behind you.

True leadership starts with a "yes." It shows up in everyday choices, such as encouraging someone who feels left out, standing up for what's right, starting something that matters, or simply setting an example through how you live.

If God has placed a mission on your heart, don't hold back. He believes in you.

He'll equip you, and He'll be with you every step of the way.

Reflection Questions

- Have you ever felt too small, quiet, or unsure to lead, even when you sensed God nudging you?
- What is one area (at home, school, church, or online) where God might be calling you to lead with quiet courage?
- What's one step you can take this week to lead not from fear, but from faith?

(Leadership often starts with one brave yes. Let this be yours.)

Prayer

God,

Thank You for calling ordinary people to do extraordinary things.

When I feel scared or unsure, remind me that You are with me.

Help me listen to Your voice and lead with Your courage, not my own.

Make me bold for the things You ask me to do.

Amen.

Faith Challenge

Think of one way you can lead by example this week:

Maybe standing up for someone who feels alone.

Maybe speaking kindly when others gossip.

Maybe inviting someone new into your group.

Big leadership starts with small acts of courage.

Chapter 11: Gideon — God's Strength in Your Weakness

Have you ever felt like you weren't strong enough, smart enough, or brave enough to do something big? Maybe you looked at what God was asking you to do and thought, *"There's no way I can do this."*

Gideon felt the same way, but his story shows that when you trust God, **your weakness becomes the perfect place for His strength to shine.**

The Bible Story (Judges 6-7, Retold)

Israel again turned away from the Lord. They broke His covenant and worshiped idols. In response, God gave them into the hand of Midian for seven years (Judges 6:1). The Midianites raided their fields, destroyed their crops, and left the people hiding in caves.

Gideon was threshing wheat in secret when the angel of the Lord appeared and said, "The Lord is with you, O mighty man of valor" (Judges 6:12). Gideon did not see himself that way. He answered, "My clan is the weakest... and I am the least in my father's house" (Judges 6:15). But God said, "I will be with you" (Judges 6:16).

Gideon asked for signs. First, fire consumed an offering (Judges 6:21). Then came the fleece—wet one day, dry the next (Judges 6:36-40). God gave every answer.

When the time came to fight, Gideon assembled an army. But God said there were too many men. He reduced the army from thousands to three hundred (Judges 7:2-7). God did not want Israel to claim the victory by their own strength.

At night, Gideon and the three hundred surrounded the camp. They broke jars, blew trumpets, and shouted as God commanded. The Midianites fled in confusion. The battle ended before swords were drawn (Judges 7:20-22).

But the real point wasn't Gideon's bravery. It was about God. God used weakness to show His strength. He used a hesitant man to display His power. The victory was about reminding Israel that their God already was.

Takeaway: God Uses the Small and the Scared

You might feel like you don't have enough courage, strength or skills. But when you trust God, you have **more than enough**. God isn't looking for people who are already powerful. He's looking for people who are willing to trust His power. Your weakness is not a problem for God, it's an opportunity for His greatness to show through your life.

When you feel small, remember: **You plus God is always bigger than anything you face.**

Reflection Questions

- When have you felt too small or too weak for something big?
- How would it change your thinking if you truly believed God's strength could work through you?

Prayer

God,

Sometimes I feel like I'm not enough.

Thank You for reminding me that with You, I have everything I need.

Help me trust Your strengths instead of focusing on my weaknesses.

Use my life to show Your greatness to the world.

Amen.

Faith Challenge

Pick one thing today that scares you. Something you've been avoiding because you feel too small. Pray about it. Then, take one small step forward, trusting that God will meet you there with His strength.

Chapter 12: Ruth — Loyalty That Changes Everything

Have you ever had a friend or family member who needed you and you had to decide whether to stay or walk away? Choosing to stay loyal isn't always easy. It can mean sticking with someone even when it's hard. The story of Ruth shows us the kind of loyalty that changes lives.

The Bible Story (Ruth 1–4, Retold)

Ruth wasn't born into a family that worshiped God. She grew up in a land called Moab, where people followed different gods. But one day, Ruth married into a family from Israel, people who believed in the one true God.

Through them, Ruth got to know about God's love and faithfulness. Then disaster hit. Ruth's husband died. So did her father-in-law and brother-in-law.

All that was left were Ruth, her sister-in-law, and her mother-in-law, Naomi. Three women. Alone. With no protection, no money, no easy future. Naomi, heartbroken, decided to go back to her hometown in Israel. She told Ruth and her sister-in-law to go back to their own families, to start over. One sister-in-law left.

But Ruth refused. She said: **"Where you go, I will go. Where you stay, I will stay.**

Your people will be my people, and your God will be my God." (Ruth 1:16)

Ruth gave up everything to stay with Naomi. Life wasn't easy for them in Israel. Ruth worked hard gathering leftover grain from fields just to keep them fed. But God saw Ruth's loyalty, and He honored it.

Ruth caught the attention of a kind man named Boaz, who later married her. Together, they became part of the family line that would lead all the way to King David, and eventually to Jesus.

Ruth's loyalty didn't just change her life. It changed history.

Takeaway: Loyalty Reflects God's Heart

Real love doesn't quit when things get hard.

Real loyalty stays when it would be easier to walk away.

In a world where people are quick to abandon friendships, families, and even faith when it gets tough, God calls us to something deeper.

When you stand by someone with love and loyalty, you reflect the very heart of God.

God never gives up on you.

He is always faithful.

And when you stay loyal, even when it's hard, you show His kind of love to the world.

Small acts of loyalty can lead to bigger plans than you could ever imagine.

Reflection Questions

- When have you had to make a choice to stay loyal to someone, even when it was hard?
- Can you think of a time when something in your life felt broken or hopeless, but later, you saw how God brought something good out of it?

Prayer

God,

Thank You for never giving up on me.

Help me be loyal and loving like You.

Show me where I can stand by someone who needs me.

Teach me to love with a heart that reflects Your faithfulness.

Amen.

Faith Challenge

Think of one person you can encourage today by being loyal. Maybe it's a friend going through something hard or a family member who needs your support.

Reach out, help them, pray for them and show them they aren't alone. Loyalty isn't just a feeling. It's an action that changes lives.

Chapter 13: Samuel's Calling — Hearing God's Voice

Have you ever wondered if God actually speaks to people today?

Maybe you've thought, *"If God wants me to do something, how will I know?"*

Hearing God's voice can feel mysterious.

But the story of Samuel shows us that God still speaks — and He often speaks to young hearts who are willing to listen.

The Bible Story (1 Samuel 3, Retold)

Samuel was just a boy when God called him.

He lived in the temple, serving under a priest named Eli. But it was a spiritually dark time for Israel. People had turned away from God, and His voice had grown quiet. The Bible says that in those days, "the word of the Lord was rare" [1 Samuel 3:1]. Not because God had changed but because the people had stopped listening.

One night, as Samuel was sleeping, he heard a voice call out:

"Samuel!"

He jumped up and ran to Eli.

"Here I am! You called me!"

But Eli said, "I didn't call you. Go back to bed."

Samuel went back to sleep.

Again, he heard it: "Samuel!"

He ran to Eli again. "I'm here! You called me!" But Eli shook his head. "I didn't call you, my son. Lie down again."

This happened a third time. Finally, Eli realized what was happening: God was calling Samuel.

Eli gave him new instructions: "If you hear the voice again, say, 'Speak, Lord, for Your servant is listening.'"

So Samuel went back to bed. Sure enough, the voice came again: "Samuel! Samuel!"

This time, Samuel answered just like Eli told him: "Speak, Lord, for Your servant is listening" (1 Samuel 3:10).

That night, God spoke to Samuel for the first time, and many more times after that. Samuel grew up to be one of the greatest prophets in Israel's history. He anointed kings, spoke truth boldly, and helped turn the hearts of the people back toward God.

But it all started with one simple response: "I'm listening."

Takeaway: God Still Speaks, and He Wants You to Hear

God isn't silent. He still speaks to us today through His Word, through prayer, through wise people He places in our lives, and sometimes through a quiet stirring in our hearts.

But here's the truth: Samuel wasn't just an ordinary listener. He was called to be a prophet, a person God chose to speak through in a very specific way to lead His people (1 Samuel 3:20).

That role was unique, and not everyone hears from God like Samuel did. Still, there's something powerful we can learn from him.

Samuel was young. He didn't have everything figured out. But his heart was open. When God called, he didn't run or argue. He simply said, "Speak, Lord. I'm listening."

You don't have to be perfect or spiritually elite to tune your heart toward God. You just have to be humble and willing to respond.

Reflection Questions

- Have you ever felt like God was trying to get your attention?
- How can you make more space in your life to listen for God's voice?

Prayer

God,

I want to hear You.

I want to know Your voice.

Help me slow down and listen when You are speaking.

Teach me to follow wherever You lead.

I am ready to say, "Speak, Lord. I'm listening."

Amen.

Faith Challenge

Find a quiet space today, even if you have just five minutes. Turn off your phone, music, and distractions.

Pray this simple prayer: *"God, speak. I'm listening."* Then sit quietly. Don't rush. Sometimes the most powerful moments come in silence.

Chapter 14: David and Goliath — Be Strong, Even When You're Small

Have you ever faced something that felt way too big for you? Maybe it was a huge problem at school, a broken friendship, a dream that seemed impossible, or a fear that kept growing inside you. You looked at it and thought, *"I'm just one person. What can I do?"*

David knew what that felt like. But he also knew something bigger: That with God, you are never too small to make a difference.

The Bible Story (1 Samuel 17, Retold)

The army of Israel was stuck. Across the valley, the enemy army had a giant warrior named Goliath. He was over nine feet tall, covered in heavy armor, and had been fighting for years.

Every day, Goliath stood in the field and shouted: "Who will fight me? Send someone! If you win, we will be your servants. But if I win, you will be ours."

Everyone was terrified.

One day, a teenager named David showed up. He wasn't a soldier. He was a shepherd, a kid who spent his days protecting sheep from wild animals.

David heard Goliath's challenge, and he heard something else too: the fear in Israel's army.

David didn't see just a giant. He saw someone insulting God.

David trusted God more than he feared Goliath. He said to the king: "I'll fight him."

The king tried to dress David in heavy armor, but it didn't fit. David took it off and picked up what he knew best: his slingshot and five smooth stones. He stepped out into the field with only his faith and his courage.

Goliath laughed. But David wasn't laughing.

He said:

"You come against me with sword and spear, but I come against you in the name of the Lord." (1 Samuel 17:45)

David slung one stone at the giant. The stone hit Goliath right between the eyes. The giant crashed to the ground.

David won, not because he was the strongest, but because he trusted God with everything he had.

Takeaway: You Are Stronger Than You Think

David didn't win that battle to prove how brave *he* was. He stood in the gap for God's people and God brought the victory.

In the same way, Jesus stands in the gap for us. He doesn't just help us face our battles: He's already won the one we couldn't.

Where we were afraid, He was faithful. Where we were weak, He was victorious.

The story of David and Goliath isn't first about us being brave. It's about trusting the One who fights on our behalf.

Reflection Questions

- What's one "giant" you're facing right now?
- What would it look like to face that giant with **God's strength**, instead of relying on your own?
- What small, bold step could you take today to say: "I trust You, God, even here"?

(You don't have to feel brave to act in faith. Courage is showing up anyway, knowing God stands with you.)

Prayer

God,

Sometimes the problems I face feel way too big.

Sometimes I feel too small to make a difference.

Help me trust You like David did.

Give me the courage to step forward with faith, knowing You fight for me.

Amen.

Faith Challenge

Identify one "giant" in your life today.

Write it down.

Next to it, write this sentence:

"God is bigger than this."

Pray about it.

Then take one small action step forward — even if it feels scary.

You might be small, but you stand with the God who never loses.

Chapter 15: Elijah Runs and Hears God — God Speaks in the Quiet

Have you ever felt like running away from everything? Like the pressure is too much... the fear too big... and you're just done?

You're not the only one. Even Elijah, one of the greatest prophets in the Bible, reached a breaking point.

He had just seen a huge miracle, but then fear rushed in, and he ran for his life. What happened next is one of the most tender, honest moments in all of Scripture and it shows us something powerful about how God speaks.

The Bible Story (1 Kings 19, Retold)

Elijah was a prophet, a messenger sent by God to speak truth to a nation that had stopped listening. At the time, Israel was worshiping a false god named **Baal**, a fake deity people prayed to for rain and their crops, among others. Elijah stood almost alone in defending the one true God.

In a dramatic showdown on Mount Carmel, Elijah challenged 450 prophets of Baal. They called on their god all day and nothing happened. Then Elijah prayed once, and God answered with fire from heaven. Everyone saw it. The crowd fell on their faces in awe. It was a huge victory for God.

But not everyone celebrated. When Queen Jezebel heard what happened, she was furious. She sent Elijah a threat: "You're going to die." Elijah panicked. He ran for his life into the wilderness. Exhausted, he collapsed under a tree and prayed, "God, I've had enough. Let me die."

He felt completely alone. Afraid. Burned out.

But God didn't scold him. He didn't send a lecture or lightning. Instead, God sent an angel with food and let Elijah sleep. Twice.

Then God led Elijah to Mount Horeb, the same mountain where He had once spoken to Moses. There, Elijah hid in a cave. And God asked him a question, not once, but twice:

"What are you doing here, Elijah?"

Elijah poured out his heart both times: "I've done everything You asked. But I'm alone. Everyone else has turned away."

Then God told Elijah to stand on the mountain. A powerful wind tore through. Then an earthquake. Then fire.

But God wasn't in any of those.

Finally, there came a **gentle whisper**, a low, quiet sound. That's where Elijah heard God's presence.

God didn't just comfort Elijah. He gave him clear direction: "Go back. You're not finished yet."

God told him to anoint new kings, to find Elisha as his helper, and, most importantly, to remember that he was *not* alone. God had preserved 7,000 others who had stayed faithful.

Elijah's story reminds us: God's power doesn't always show up the way we expect. But His voice is never silent.

His mission for us continues, even when we feel like giving up.

Takeaway: God Doesn't Yell — He Whispers

Sometimes, we expect God to speak through big signs and loud moments. But more often, God speaks in the quiet. In the stillness. In the whisper.

Elijah feels alone but God points out that he's not. There are 7,000 others who have not bowed to Baal. This is important today too: our feelings of isolation may be real, but they're not always true. Elijah thought he was the last faithful one. But God showed him he wasn't alone, and neither are we. Sometimes, what we feel isn't the full picture.

Reflection Questions

- Have you ever wanted to run away from something hard?
- When was the last time you sat in silence and asked God to speak?

Prayer

God,

Sometimes life feels like too much.

I feel afraid.

I feel alone.

But I believe You are still here, even in the quiet.

Help me stop running.

Help me rest in You.

And help me listen for Your whisper.

Amen.

Faith Challenge

Find a quiet space today, no noise, no screens, no music.

Set a timer for five minutes.

Just sit with God.

Pray this:

"God, I'm listening."

Then let the silence stay.

God often speaks to those who are willing to wait in stillness.

Chapter 16: King Hezekiah — Praying When Everything Falls Apart

What do you do when the news is bad and everything feels like it's falling apart? When the odds are against you, the pressure is too heavy, and you can't fix it on your own?

That's exactly where King Hezekiah found himself. He had no backup plan, no power left to lean on. But instead of giving up, he did one simple, powerful thing: He spread it all out before God , and prayed.

The Bible Story (2 Kings 18-20, Retold)

Hezekiah was king in Judah. Unlike many before him, he trusted in the Lord. He removed the high places, tore down idols, and restored worship according to the law of God (2 Kings 18:3-6).

Then came Assyria. Their army had conquered every kingdom they faced. They surrounded Jerusalem and sent a message: do not think your God will deliver you. No other nation has escaped. You will fall next (2 Kings 18:28-35).

Hezekiah did not rely on military power. He went to the temple, took the letter from the Assyrians, and laid it before the Lord. Then he prayed: "O Lord, the God of Israel... You alone are God... Incline Your ear... deliver us" (2 Kings 19:15-19).

God responded through the prophet Isaiah. The message was clear: "Thus says the Lord... He shall not come into this city... for I will defend this city to save it" (2 Kings 19:32-34).

That night, the angel of the Lord struck down one hundred eighty-five thousand in the Assyrian camp. By morning, the army was gone. The siege ended without a battle (2 Kings 19:35-36).

Later, Hezekiah became sick. Isaiah brought a word from the Lord: "Set your house in order, for you shall die" (2 Kings 20:1).

Hezekiah turned to the wall and prayed. He wept. Before Isaiah left the courtyard, God sent him back with another message: "I have heard your prayer. I will heal you... I will add fifteen years to your life" (2 Kings 20:5-6).

Hezekiah's strength was not in himself. It was in the Word of the Lord. In war and in sickness, he sought God.

In every crisis, Hezekiah didn't rely on his own strength. He relied on the Word of the Lord.

Takeaway: When You Can't Win the Battle, Exalt the One Who Can

Sometimes, life brings threats you cannot outrun. Problems too big for your plans.

Moments too heavy for your strength.

But Hezekiah didn't just ask God for rescue. He exalted God's name.

He laid the enemy's letter before the Lord and said,

"God, You alone are King. You rule over every nation. Show the world who You are."

His prayer wasn't just about relief.

It was rooted in worship.

He wanted God's greatness to be known.

And God answered.

Not just because Hezekiah was afraid. But because Hezekiah remembered who God is.

When your strength runs out, that's not failure.

That's a moment to turn your eyes upward. Not just for help but for God's glory to be seen in your story. He still responds today.

Not always in the way we imagine, but always in the way that reveals who He is.

Reflection Questions

- What is something in your life right now that feels too big or too hard to handle?
- Have you ever tried laying it out before God in prayer, like Hezekiah did?
- What would change if your first response was prayer, not panic?

Prayer

God,

Sometimes I don't know what to do.

The fear is loud.

The pressure is heavy.

But I believe You are bigger.

So I'm laying this down before You.

Help me trust that You hear me — and that You're already working.

Amen.

Faith Challenge

Write down one thing that's stressing you out.

Then, like Hezekiah, physically lay it out before God — on your desk, your bed, or in your journal.

Pray over it.

Say:

"God, I give this to You."

Then leave it in His hands.

Chapter 17: Shadrach, Meshach, and Abednego — Faith in the Fire

Have you ever felt pressured to go along with something you knew was wrong?

Maybe you were afraid that if you didn't, people would laugh at you, leave you out, or even turn against you.

Standing strong for what's right isn't easy.

But the story of Shadrach, Meshach, and Abednego shows that when you stand with God, He stands with you, even in the fire.

The Bible Story (Daniel 3, Retold)

King Nebuchadnezzar ruled over Babylon, and he built a massive golden statue. He made a law: When the music played, **everyone** had to bow down and worship the statue.

Everyone. No exceptions.

But three young men, Shadrach, Meshach, and Abednego, refused. They worshiped the one true God, and they weren't about to bow to anyone or anything else.

The king was furious. He gave them a final warning: *"Bow, or you'll be thrown into a blazing furnace."*

Their answer was strong and clear:

"The God we serve is able to save us. But even if He doesn't, we will not bow." (Daniel 3:17–18)

Even if it cost them everything.

The king ordered the furnace heated seven times hotter than normal. The fire was so fierce it killed the soldiers who threw them in. But when the king looked into the flames, he was shocked.

There weren't three men in the fire — there were four.

One of them looked like "a son of the gods."

God was with them in the fire. And when they walked out, not even their clothes smelled like smoke.

The king praised their God: The God who saves, who shows up, who honors faith that stands strong.

Takeaway: Faith Stands When the World Bows

Shadrach, Meshach, and Abednego were not just resisting a trend.

They were defying a king.

In a foreign empire that had conquered their homeland, they stood before the most powerful ruler of their time. When commanded to bow before a golden image or be burned alive, they made their choice.

They didn't obey because they were sure God would deliver them.

They obeyed because they knew God was worthy—no matter the outcome.

Their courage was not rooted in comfort. It was rooted in conviction.

They knew that no threat from a king could overpower the truth of God.

God did not prevent the fire.

He entered it.

That is who He is.

He may not always remove the trial.

But He never abandons His people in it.

Their story reminds us: God's truth is greater than any throne.

His presence is stronger than any fire.

And His glory is worth every cost.

Faith that endures under pressure is not just noticed, it is honored. Because when you stand for what is right in the face of what is wrong, you echo the courage of those who trusted God in the furnace.

Reflection Questions

- Have you ever felt pressured to do something you knew wasn't right — just to fit in? What did you do?
- What would it look like to trust God boldly — even if it meant standing out or standing alone?
- Do you act in loyalty because of promise of reward or outcome or because it comes out of truth?

Prayer

God,

Give me the courage to stand strong when I feel pressured to bow to the wrong things.

Remind me that You are always with me, even when the fire feels hot.

Help me live boldly for You, no matter what others think.

Thank You for being the God who never leaves my side.

Amen.

Faith Challenge

Think about one area where you are tempted to "bow down" — to fit in, to stay quiet, to blend in.

Pray for strength today to stand strong, even if it feels hard.

Remember: you are never standing alone.

Chapter 18: Daniel in the Lion's Den — Trust When You're Surrounded

Have you ever felt trapped in a situation where doing the right thing seemed risky? Maybe you knew speaking up for your faith or your values would cost you friends, opportunities, or respect.

It's not easy to stand firm when you feel surrounded. Daniel knows exactly how that feels, and his story shows that even when you're surrounded by danger, **God is closer than you think.**

The Bible Story (Daniel 6, Retold)

Daniel had spent years serving as a leader in Babylon. He was known for being wise, honest, and faithful.

Even when he lived far from his home and among people who didn't believe in his God, Daniel stayed true.

Some of the other leaders were jealous. They didn't like how much the king respected Daniel. So, they came up with a sneaky plan.

They convinced the king to sign a law saying that **for thirty days**, no one could pray to any god or person except the king himself. Anyone who disobeyed would be thrown into a den of hungry lions.

Daniel heard about the law. He knew the risk. He knew what could happen. But Daniel didn't hide.

He went to his window, just like he always did, and prayed to God openly. The jealous leaders caught him and ran to tell the king.

The king, who liked Daniel, was heartbroken. But the law could not be undone. Daniel was thrown into the lion's den.

The stone was rolled across the entrance. It looked like the end.

But in the middle of the night, God sent an angel to shut the lions' mouths. When the king rushed to the den in the morning, he called out: "Daniel! Has your God saved you?"

And Daniel's voice answered back:

"My God sent His angel, and He shut the mouths of the lions." (Daniel 6:22)

Daniel was pulled out, completely unharmed. And the king praised Daniel's God, recognizing His power and greatness.

Takeaway: Trust God, Even When You Feel Surrounded

Daniel's story showed us this: our hope is in the God who holds all power, sees every act of obedience, and walks with His people through every trial.

God's presence was with Daniel and His glory was made known because Daniel stood firm.

T

hat same God still reigns.

You may not face lions, but you will face moments that feel risky. In those moments, don't trust your circumstances. Trust the One who is worthy.

Reflection Questions

- Have you ever felt surrounded by pressure to hide your faith, change who you are, or stay quiet about what you believe?
- What does it look like to keep trusting God in moments when everything feels risky or uncertain?
- Is there a "lion's den" moment in your life where you need to remember: **God is with me here**?

(Your courage doesn't have to roar — it just has to trust. God handles the lions.)

Prayer

God,

When I feel trapped, scared, or surrounded, remind me that You are bigger than anything I face.

Give me the courage to keep trusting You, even when it feels dangerous or lonely.

Help me stand strong and know that You are with me every step of the way.

Amen.

Faith Challenge

This week, choose one small way to stand strong for your faith:

- Praying openly.
- Standing up for what's right.
- Choosing honesty when it's hard.

Every brave step strengthens your faith — and shows others the strength of your God.

Chapter 19: Esther — You Were Born for This Moment

Have you ever felt caught between wanting to do what's right and being afraid of what might happen if you do?

Doing the right thing can feel risky. It can feel scary. But sometimes, you are exactly where you are for a reason and your courage can change everything.

That's the story of Esther.

The Bible Story (Esther 1–10, Retold)

Esther was a young Jewish girl living in exile under the rule of the Persian Empire. Her people had been conquered, scattered, and were now a minority under foreign kings. They had no power. No homeland. No protection.

One day, the king of Persia decided he needed a new queen. Esther was chosen—not because of her background, but because of her beauty. She kept her identity as a Jew hidden, just as her cousin Mordecai advised. In a foreign palace, surrounded by wealth and luxury, it would have been easy for her to stay silent.

But then came a crisis. A powerful official named Haman convinced the king to sign a decree that would wipe out all the Jews in the empire. Esther's people. Her family. Her heritage.

Mordecai sent word to Esther: "You must speak to the king."

But that wasn't simple. In Persia, approaching the king without an invitation, even as queen, could mean death. Esther hesitated. She was afraid. But Mordecai's reply was clear:

"Who knows if you were made queen for such a time as this?" (Esther 4:14)

Maybe God had placed Esther in this exact position, at this exact moment, for a greater purpose. Esther prayed. She fasted. Then she stepped into the throne room, risking everything.

The king listened. The plot was exposed. The Jews were saved. But this story isn't just about Esther's courage.

It's about God's hidden hand—guiding, protecting, and preserving His people, even when His name isn't mentioned once in the book.

God kept His covenant. He protected His people and He used Esther to do it. Even when God seems silent, He was never absent.

Takeaway: You Are Where You Are for a Reason

Sometimes, God positions you in just the right place at just the right time even if it feels uncertain, uncomfortable, or unnoticed.

That was true for Esther, but over time, through prayer, waiting, listening, and trusting, she stepped into what God had prepared.

Her courage wasn't about a single dramatic moment. It was a slow, steady faith, a willingness to risk everything for the good of others and the glory of God.

You may not have a throne or a kingdom, but you do have opportunities.

God often works behind the scenes, just like He did in Esther's story. He's still writing stories today through people like you.

So, if you're in a hard place, don't assume it's pointless. If you feel unseen, don't believe you're forgotten. You are where you are for a reason.

God can use your faithfulness even if no one sees it but Him.

Reflection Questions

- Have you ever had a moment where you had to choose between staying comfortable or doing what was right? What happened?
- Where in your life right now might God be nudging you to be brave, speak truth, or take a stand?
- What challenges will you allow yourself to welcome and apply?

(God sees the full picture — and He put you here for a reason. Don't be afraid to be bold.)

Prayer

> *God,*
>
> *Sometimes it's hard to be brave.*
>
> *Help me remember that You have a purpose for where I am and who I am.*
>
> *Give me the courage to stand up for what's right, even when it feels risky.*
>
> *Help me trust that You are with me in every step I take.*
>
> *Amen.*

Faith Challenge

Look around your life today.

Is there someone who needs you to stand with them?

Is there a place where you could speak up for what's right?

Take one small brave step today.

You never know how much your courage could mean to someone else — or to God's bigger plan.

Section 3: Returning to God — Mercy and Second Chances (Job – Jonah)

Sometimes life breaks you. Sometimes **you** do something wrong.

Maybe it's a mistake you made, a dream that collapsed, or a time when you ran the opposite direction from what you knew was right. This part of the Bible is for those moments.

In these stories, we meet people who felt angry, afraid, unqualified, or completely undone. Yet, they were never abandoned. Job teaches us how to keep trusting when everything falls apart. Nehemiah shows how God helps rebuild what's broken. Jonah reminds us that even when we run, God runs after us.

This section is all about second chances, divine comebacks, and the truth that God's love doesn't give up when we do.

Chapter 20: Job — Faith in the Middle of Pain

Have you ever wondered, *"Why is this happening to me?"*

Maybe you worked hard for something and still lost. Maybe you prayed for something important and it didn't happen.

It's a hard place to be and it's easy to wonder if God sees you or even cares.

But you're not the first to ask those questions. Job asked them too, and his story shows us what real faith looks like when everything falls apart.

The Bible Story (Job 1-42, Retold)

Job had a good life. He was honest, kind, and faithful to God. He had a big family, lots of land, and many blessings.

Then, almost overnight, Job lost everything.

His animals were stolen or killed. His servants were attacked. His children died in a terrible accident. And then Job himself became very sick.

Pain piled on pain.

Loss piled on loss.

His friends came to visit him, but instead of comforting him, they told him he must have done something wrong to deserve all this. Even his own wife said, "Just curse God and die."

But Job refused to give up on God.

He didn't pretend everything was fine, he cried out. He poured out his sadness, his anger, his confusion. He asked the hard questions. He didn't hide his pain.

Through it all, Job never walked away from God. He kept praying. He kept wrestling.

He kept believing that somehow, God was still good even when he didn't understand.

In the end, God spoke to Job with a reminder of His power, His wisdom, and His love.

God restored Job's life, giving him even more blessings than before. But the real miracle wasn't the blessings. The real miracle was Job's faith that survived the storm.

Takeaway: Real Faith Holds On, Even in the Hardest Times

Faith is **choosing to stay close to God**, even when nothing makes sense.

Job's life fell apart. He lost everything: his family, his health, his home.

And he didn't stay silent.

He cried.

He questioned.

He struggled.

But he never let go of God.

That's what real faith looks like.

Not a perfect smile — but a decision to **cling to God through the pain**.

It's okay to wrestle.

It's okay to feel broken.

It's okay to not understand.

What matters is that you **don't walk away**.

Because even when it feels like God is silent, He is still present.

Even when everything hurts, He is still holding you.

And even when your heart is breaking, He is building something stronger within you — something deeper than surface-level faith.

Pain doesn't mean God has abandoned you.

It might actually be the place where your faith grows roots that hold, no matter the storm.

Reflection Questions

- Have you ever walked through a time when life felt unfair, painful, or confusing — like Job?
- During that time, how did you respond to God? Did you draw closer, pull away, or feel stuck in between?
- What would it look like to say, even now: "God, I don't understand — but I'm not letting go"?

(Let this be the moment you hold on. You're not alone in your questions — or your faith.)

Prayer

God,

Sometimes life hurts so much I don't even know what to say.

Help me trust You even when I don't understand what's happening.

Give me the strength to hold on to You in the middle of the storm.

Remind me that You love me, even when I can't feel it.

Amen.

Faith Challenge

If you're going through something hard right now, take a few minutes to write out a prayer to God.

Be honest.

Tell Him your real feelings.

Then, at the bottom of your prayer, write this:

"God, I trust You. Even now."

Keep that prayer somewhere close.

Every time the pain feels heavy, go back and read it again.

Let it remind you: your faith is bigger than your pain.

Chapter 21: Nehemiah — Building Dreams with God's Help

Have you ever had a dream or goal that felt too big to reach? Maybe it was starting something new. Fixing something broken. Helping someone when it seemed too hard.

You knew it mattered but you also knew you couldn't do it alone.

Nehemiah had a dream like that. Through his story, we learn that when God calls you to build something, He also gives you the strength to finish it.

The Bible Story (Nehemiah 1-6, Retold)

Nehemiah wasn't a soldier or a famous leader. He was a cupbearer, someone who served drinks to the king of Persia and made sure they were safe.

But one day, Nehemiah heard devastating news. The walls around Jerusalem, his people's city, were broken down. The gates were burned. The people who lived there were weak, scared, and ashamed.

Nehemiah's heart broke.

He cried.

He fasted.

He prayed.

Then, even though he wasn't a warrior or a builder, Nehemiah felt God calling him to do something about it. He asked the king for permission to go rebuild the walls. The king said yes.

When Nehemiah got to Jerusalem, he didn't find an easy job. He found rubble. He found enemies who laughed at him, threatened him, and tried to stop the work.

But Nehemiah didn't quit.

He organized the people. He gave them tools and weapons. He encouraged them when they were tired.

And in just 52 days — with God's help — they rebuilt the broken walls of the city.

Nehemiah's faith and courage turned ruins into strength.

Takeaway: If God Gives You a Dream, He'll Help You Build It

God often calls ordinary people to do extraordinary things. Not because they are powerful, but because they trust Him.

When God gives you a dream it's going to take work.

It's going to face opposition.

You might even want to quit sometimes.

But remember: God doesn't give dreams without also giving the strength, the courage, and the help to see them through.

You aren't building alone. God is with you every step of the way. Don't quit just because it's hard. Big dreams are always built one small step at a time.

Reflection Questions

- What is one dream or goal you feel God has put on your heart?
- What small step could you take today toward building that dream?

Prayer

God,

Sometimes the dreams You give me feel too big and too hard.

Help me trust that You will help me build what You have called me to start.

Give me courage when I'm tired.

Give me strength when I feel small.

Help me stay faithful, step by step.

Amen.

Faith Challenge

Write down one dream, goal, or mission you feel pulled toward, even if it feels impossible right now.

Pray over it today.

Then write one action step you can take this week, no matter how small.

Building big things starts with one small yes.

Chapter 22: Jonah — Running from God's Call

Have you ever known you should do something but ran the other way instead? Maybe you felt a nudge to apologize, help someone, or take a risk, but fear, pride, or comfort got in the way.

Jonah did the same thing, but his story shows us that even when we run, God doesn't give up on us.

The Bible Story (Jonah 1-4, Retold)

One day, God gave Jonah a mission: "Go to the city of Nineveh. Tell the people there to stop doing evil and turn back to Me."

Nineveh was a scary place. The people there were known for being violent and cruel.

Jonah didn't want to go.

So, instead of obeying, Jonah ran away. He got on a ship sailing in the opposite direction.

A huge storm hit the sea. Waves crashed. The sailors on the boat panicked, throwing cargo overboard to stay afloat.

Finally, Jonah admitted he was the problem. He told them to throw him into the sea to calm the storm. Reluctantly, they did.

The moment Jonah hit the water, the sea grew calm.

God, in His mercy, sent a giant fish to swallow Jonah — not to punish him, but to save him.

Inside the belly of the fish, Jonah prayed.

He cried out to God with a heart full of regret, and after three days, the fish spit him out onto dry land.

This time, when God said, "Go to Nineveh," Jonah obeyed. He preached to the people, warning them to turn back to God.

They listened and repented. They changed their ways, and God showed them mercy.

Jonah wasn't perfect. He struggled with anger, pride, and fear, but God still used him to make a huge difference.

Takeaway: God's Mercy is Bigger

God told Jonah to go to Nineveh — a brutal, violent city. He didn't run because he was scared. He ran because he didn't want them to be saved.

Jonah knew God was merciful. That was the problem. He didn't think the Ninevites deserved it.

So, he got on a boat in the opposite direction. But God didn't abandon Jonah.

He pursued him — not to punish, but to restore. Even in Jonah's rebellion, God was working.

Even after his resistance, God gave him another chance to obey.

That same mercy is offered to us. Maybe you've resisted something God asked of you. Maybe you've let bitterness, pride, or comfort guide your steps.

It's not too late.

God's calling may stretch you. It may challenge what you think people deserve. But it will always lead toward redemption — for you and for others.

God's mercy is bigger than your mistakes. Bigger than your opinions. And always worth saying yes to.

Reflection Questions

- Is there something you feel God might be calling you to do that you're avoiding?
- How has this story inspired you to look differently at forgiveness?

Prayer

God,

Thank You for never giving up on me.

Even when I run or hide, You keep loving me.

Give me the courage to say yes to the things You call me to do.

Help me trust that Your plans are good, even when they feel scary.

Amen.

Faith Challenge

Think about one thing you know deep down God might be calling you to do, big or small.

It could be helping someone, forgiving someone, standing up for something right. Pray about it today.

Then take one step toward obedience even if it feels hard. God's plans are always better than your fears.

Section 4: Encountering Jesus — Love That Transforms (Matthew-John)

When Jesus entered the world, everything changed. He didn't come as a king in a castle, but as a baby in a manger, quiet, humble, and full of promise. From that moment on, lives began to shift.

This part of the Bible follows the life of Jesus, from His birth to His resurrection, and shows what happens when ordinary people meet an extraordinary Savior.

Some were sick. Some were outcasts. Some were caught in sin. Others were just curious or confused. But every single person who encountered Jesus came away changed because He met them with truth, love, and compassion.

These stories remind us that Jesus still meets us the same way today: personally, powerfully, and full of grace. When you truly encounter Him, your life will never be the same.

Chapter 23: Birth of Jesus — Hope in the Hard Times

Have you ever known a moment when everything felt dark?

That kind of darkness is not new.

From the beginning, humanity chose rebellion. Sin entered the world, and with it came separation from God. Pain, injustice, fear, and death followed. Darkness became the condition of the human heart (Genesis 3; Romans 5:12).

But God did not leave the world in that condition. He made a promise. Through the prophet Isaiah, He declared that those who walk in darkness would see a great light (Isaiah 9:2). That promise was not vague. It pointed to a Savior who would undo what sin had broken.

The fulfillment came in Jesus Christ. His birth was not just a sign of hope. It was the arrival of the Light of the World (John 8:12). In Him, the darkness could not remain.

The birth of Jesus is not sentimental. It is necessary. Without Him, there is no rescue. Without Him, there is no peace. He did not come to make life easier. He came to save the lost.

The light still shines. Not because the world is better, but because Christ is risen.

The Bible Story (Luke 2:1-20, Retold)

A long time ago, in a land ruled by a powerful empire, the people of Israel were waiting. They were longing for the promised Messiah.

The One who would fulfill God's covenant, rescue them from sin and death, and bring lasting peace.

And then, in the quiet of night, in a small town called Bethlehem, that promise was fulfilled.

Not with royal banners.

Not in a palace.

But in a stable.

The eternal Son of God, fully divine, fully human, entered the world as a newborn child.

His parents, Mary and Joseph, had traveled a long way to Bethlehem because of a government census. When they arrived, there was no room left for them anywhere.

Only a stable where animals stayed. And there, in the humblest of places, **Jesus Christ** was born.

Mary wrapped Him in cloth and laid Him in a manger because that was all they had.

Nearby, shepherds were out in the fields watching over their sheep. Suddenly, the night sky lit up as an angel appeared.

The angel spoke:

"Do not be afraid. I bring you good news that will bring great joy to all people.

Today, in the town of David, a Savior has been born to you; He is Christ the Lord." [Luke 2:10-11]

Then, a multitude of angels filled the sky, praising God with songs of glory. The shepherds didn't wait. They ran to see what God had done.

And there they found Him — the promised King, lying in a manger.

They left rejoicing, spreading the news.

The hope of the world had come.

Not just to bring comfort.

But to bring salvation.

Takeaway: God's Light Always Breaks Through

If you're walking through darkness — doubt, depression, family hurt, or deep grief — know this: You are not forgotten. You are not beyond reach.

Jesus came for you and the light He brings is not temporary.

One day, that light will fill the whole world when Christ returns, wipes every tear, and makes all things new (Revelation 21:23-25).

The light wins.

Not because life gets easier. But because Jesus reigns — now and forever.

Reflection Questions

- When you think about the story of Jesus being born in a manger, how does it shape the way you view God's closeness to people who feel unseen or overlooked?

- Jesus came as both Savior and King. What does it mean to you personally that God's rescue plan began with a baby in a feeding trough?

Prayer

God,

Thank You for sending Jesus into a broken world to bring light and hope.

When I feel stuck in fear or sadness, remind me that You are near.

Help me trust that Your love is stronger than anything I face.

Fill my heart with hope today.

Amen.

Faith Challenge

Think of someone you know who might be going through a hard time.

Write them a short message of encouragement today — even just a few words like,

"You are not alone. God loves you."

Sharing hope with someone else can remind you of the hope you have too.

Chapter 24: The Woman Who Touched Jesus's Robe — Faith That Reaches Out

Have you ever been desperate for help, but felt too afraid to reach out? Maybe you thought, *"Why would God care about someone like me?"*

There's a story about a woman who reached out to Jesus in the middle of a huge crowd and it shows that even the smallest step of faith matters deeply to Him.

The Bible Story (Luke 8:40–48, Retold)

Jesus was on His way to help a very important man's daughter who was sick. The crowds were pressing in all around Him — pushing, shouting, grabbing.

In the middle of all that noise and movement was a woman who had been suffering for **twelve years**. She had a bleeding illness that no doctor could fix. Because of her condition, she wasn't just sick, she was considered **unclean** by her community.

She wasn't supposed to touch anyone and she wasn't supposed to be near crowds.

But she had heard about Jesus. She thought, *"If I can just touch the edge of His robe, I will be healed."*

She didn't want to make a scene and she didn't want to stop Him.

She just reached out quietly, secretly, desperate for hope.

When she touched His robe, instantly, her bleeding stopped. Her body was healed.

Jesus stopped. He asked:

"Who touched Me?" (Luke 8:45)

The crowd denied it.

Peter said,

"Everyone is touching You, Jesus!"

But Jesus knew. He had felt healing power go out from Him.

Trembling, the woman came forward and told her whole story. Jesus didn't scold her. He didn't shame her.

He said:

"Daughter, your faith has healed you. Go in peace." (Luke 8:48)

Takeaway: Even the Smallest Step of Faith Matters

The woman didn't have a perfect plan. She didn't make a big scene. She was hurting, tired, and probably felt invisible.

But she had just enough courage to do one thing: **reach out to Jesus.** She believed that even a touch could change everything.

And it did.

Jesus honored her faith and He called her "daughter."

You don't need a bold speech or flawless words to get God's attention.

You just need to reach out in faith.

A whispered prayer.

A quiet moment of surrender.

A small choice to trust.

God notices all of it.

He meets you in the quiet.

He sees what others miss.

And when you reach for Him — even shakily — He responds with healing, peace, and love that goes deeper than words.

Reflection Questions

- Have you ever felt too small, unimportant, or unworthy to bring something to God? What made you feel that way?

- What is one area of your life where you need healing, hope, or help — and what would it look like to reach out to Jesus with even a tiny step of faith today?

- What might change if you believed Jesus sees and honors even your quietest acts of trust?

(He's not looking for perfect strength — just a heart willing to reach.)

Prayer

Jesus,

Thank You for seeing my small, quiet prayers.

Thank You for caring about every part of my life — even the parts I try to hide.

Give me the courage to reach out to You, trusting that Your love is always enough.

Heal my heart.

Grow my faith.

Amen.

Faith Challenge

Today, take one small step of faith:

- Pray about something you've been too afraid to bring to God.
- Talk to someone you trust about a struggle.
- Trust Jesus with something you feel is too broken.

Even small steps toward Jesus are powerful.

Chapter 25: Jesus Feeds the 5,000 — Trusting God with What You Have

In the feeding of the 5,000, Jesus didn't just meet a need —He revealed His divine power and authority.

With just a few loaves and fish, He showed that **He is enough**. The miracle was about who Jesus is: the Son of God who satisfies completely.

The Bible Story (John 6:1–14, Retold)

Huge crowds were following Jesus. Everywhere He went, people wanted to hear Him teach, see miracles, and feel His love.

One day, a massive crowd — **more than 5,000 people** — gathered to listen. They stayed so long that it got late, and people were hungry.

Jesus asked His disciple Philip,

"Where can we buy bread to feed all these people?"

Philip panicked.

"It would take months of wages to buy enough food!"

Andrew, another disciple, spoke up:

"There's a boy here with five small loaves of bread and two fish. But what good is that for so many?"

It seemed like nothing. Way too small for the huge need.

But Jesus smiled. He told everyone to sit down. He took the boy's little lunch. He gave thanks to God.

And then He began to pass it out. The bread and fish multiplied. Everyone ate **until they were full.**

Afterward, they gathered twelve baskets full of leftovers.

Twelve baskets — from one boy's tiny lunch.

Takeaway: Jesus is Enough

The feeding of the five thousand wasn't about human effort. It wasn't about someone having the perfect plan or a generous heart.

It was about Jesus and who He is. When the crowd was hungry, it was Jesus who provided.

Not just with food for their bodies, but with a sign pointing to something deeper.

He is the Bread of Life: the only One who satisfies the hunger of the soul.

Reflection Questions

- When you think about Jesus being the "Bread of Life," what do you think that means for your everyday needs — not just physically, but spiritually and emotionally?
- How might trusting in Jesus as your true provider change the way you approach stress, success, or even your sense of identity?

Prayer

Jesus,

Sometimes I feel like I don't have much to offer.

But You remind me that small things become big when I trust You.

Take what I have — my time, my talents, my heart — and use them to bless others.

I trust You to multiply what I bring.

Amen.

Faith Challenge

Pick one "small thing" this week to offer to God:

- An encouraging text to a friend.
- A few minutes helping someone.
- A small act of kindness.

Trust that God can use it in ways bigger than you can see.

Chapter 26: Peter Walks on Water — Keeping Your Eyes on Jesus

Have you ever started something brave but then fear crept in and made you doubt yourself? Maybe you stepped out in faith, but once things got scary, you thought, *"I can't do this!"*

Peter knows exactly how that feels. His story reminds us that when fear rises, **the key is to keep your eyes on Jesus.**

The Bible Story (Matthew 14:22–33, Retold)

After a long day of teaching and miracles, Jesus sent His disciples ahead of Him, across the lake in a boat. Meanwhile, He went up a mountain to pray.

Later that night, the disciples' boat was far from shore. The wind picked up. The waves grew rough. They were struggling to move forward.

In the middle of the night, through the storm and darkness, they saw someone walking on the water toward them.

At first, they were terrified.

"It's a ghost!" they cried.

But Jesus immediately said: **"Take courage! It is I. Don't be afraid."** (Matthew 14:27)

Peter called out, *"Lord, if it's really You, tell me to come to You on the water."*

Jesus said, *"Come."*

Peter stepped out of the boat — and for a few incredible moments, he actually walked on water. But then Peter saw the wind. He felt the waves.

Fear gripped his heart and he began to sink. "Lord, save me!" he cried.

Immediately, Jesus reached out His hand and caught him. **"You of little faith,"** He said, **"why did you doubt?"** (Matthew 14:31)

When they climbed back into the boat, the wind died down. The disciples worshiped Jesus, saying, *"Truly You are the Son of God."*

Takeaway: Focus on Jesus, Not the Waves

Faith doesn't mean you'll never feel fear.

It means you know where to look **when fear shows up.**

Peter stepped out of the boat with bold faith.

He actually walked on water because his eyes were fixed on Jesus.

But the moment he shifted his focus to the storm... he started to sink.

The same thing happens to us.

Life brings problems, pressure, anxiety, doubt. It's easy to look around and feel overwhelmed.

But Jesus invites you to keep your eyes on **Him**, not on the chaos.

He doesn't expect you to be fearless. He just wants you to trust that He's **stronger than the storm.**

And even if you start to sink, even if fear wins for a moment, **Jesus is right there.**

He reaches out, holds you up, and reminds you: **You're not alone.** You don't walk on water by being perfect. You walk by focusing on the One who makes the impossible possible — and walking forward with Him.

Reflection Questions

- Have you ever stepped out in faith but fear made you hesitate or pull back? What happened?

- What would it look like for you to keep your eyes on Jesus right now?

- What simple phrase or truth can you repeat this week when fear tries to speak louder than faith?

Prayer

Jesus,

Sometimes fear feels bigger than my faith.

When the waves of life crash around me, help me keep my eyes on You.

Thank You for reaching out to catch me when I stumble.

Grow my trust, steady my heart, and lead me step by step.

Amen.

Faith Challenge

Think of one situation this week where fear is trying to pull you under.

Every time you feel fear rise, quietly pray:

"Jesus, I trust You."

Take one small step forward in faith — even if your knees are shaking.

Chapter 27: Jesus Calms the Storm — Finding Peace Inside Chaos

Have you ever felt like life was spinning out of control?

Maybe you were hit with bad news you didn't see coming.

Maybe school, friends, family, and future plans all felt like too much at once.

Maybe you just felt trapped in a storm of worry and fear, wondering if it would ever get better.

In moments like that, it's easy to think you're sinking.

But Jesus shows us that even when everything around you feels like chaos, He is still in control.

The Bible Story (Mark 4:35-41, Retold)

One evening, Jesus told His disciples, "Let's cross to the other side of the lake."

They got into a boat and started sailing. At first, everything was peaceful. But then a furious storm blew in.

Waves crashed into the boat. The wind howled. Water started filling the boat fast.

The disciples — some of them experienced fishermen — were terrified. They thought they were going to die.

Meanwhile, where was Jesus? He was asleep in the back of the boat, resting on a cushion.

In a panic, the disciples woke Him up. "Teacher! Don't you care if we drown?"

Jesus stood up.

He spoke to the storm:

"Peace. Be still." (Mark 4:39)

And just like that, the wind stopped.

The waves grew calm.

The sea became still.

Then Jesus turned to His disciples and asked: "Why are you so afraid? Do you still have no faith?" The disciples were amazed.

Even the wind and the waves obeyed Him.

Takeaway: Jesus Has Authority Over the Storm

When the disciples found themselves in a storm, they weren't just afraid of the waves.

They were overwhelmed by the realization of who was in the boat with them.

Jesus didn't calm the sea just to soothe their fear.

He did it to show them something deeper — that He is Lord over wind, waves, and all of creation.

This wasn't just a moment of peace.

It was a moment of revelation.

The disciples asked, "Who is this, that even the wind and sea obey Him?"

The answer: the Son of God.

Storms in life are real — and sometimes terrifying.

But this story doesn't promise that storms won't come.

It shows us that Jesus is not just present in the storm — He rules over it.

His power is greater than chaos.

His voice still carries authority.

And His presence is not a maybe — it's a promise.

So when life feels out of control, don't just look for peace.

Look to the One who commands the storm itself — and obeys no one but God.

Reflection Questions

- What does it mean to you that even the wind and waves obey Jesus?
- When life feels out of control, how can remembering who Jesus is help you respond differently?
- Are there areas in your life where you've been asking for peace more than seeking the presence of Christ Himself?

Prayer

Jesus,

When life feels crazy and scary, help me remember that You are bigger than any storm.

Calm my heart when I feel overwhelmed.

Teach me to trust You, even when the waves seem huge.

You are my peace, no matter what happens.

Amen.

Faith Challenge

The next time you feel overwhelmed or afraid, pause for a moment.

Close your eyes and quietly say,

"Jesus, bring Your peace."

Picture Him standing in the middle of your storm, strong and steady, speaking peace into your chaos.

You are never alone in the boat.

Chapter 28: Jesus and the Woman at the Well — Fully Known and Loved

Have you ever felt like you had to hide parts of yourself? Maybe you've messed up and felt like people wouldn't understand.

Maybe you've carried shame, loneliness, or a secret you hoped no one would see. It's easy to feel like if people really knew us, they wouldn't love us.

But Jesus shows us something different. He meets us right where we are and He loves us completely.

The Bible Story (John 4:1–26, Retold)

One day, Jesus was traveling through Samaria — a region that most Jewish people avoided.

There was a long-standing divide between Jews and Samaritans.

They disagreed about worship, history, and identity. To many Jews, Samaritans were outsiders — spiritually and culturally.

But Jesus chose to go through Samaria.

Tired from the journey, He stopped at a well around noon — the hottest part of the day.

That's when a Samaritan woman came to draw water. It was unusual. Most people came early, when it was cool and crowded. But she came alone, likely to avoid being seen or judged.

Then something even more unusual happened: Jesus — a Jewish man, a respected teacher — spoke to her. He said, "Will you give me a drink?"

This wasn't normal.

Men didn't speak openly to women like this in public, especially not rabbis. And Jews didn't speak to Samaritans, especially not with kindness.

But Jesus didn't ignore her. He didn't reject her. He engaged her. As they talked, Jesus told her something no stranger could have known — that she had been married five times, and was now living with someone who wasn't her husband.

He didn't bring this up to shame her. He brought it up to show her: He knew her. Entirely.

But the point wasn't just that Jesus saw her. It's what He revealed about Himself.

He offered her "living water" — something more satisfying than anything physical.

She asked about true worship — where and how it should happen.

And Jesus said something incredible:

"The time is coming, and has now come, when true worshipers will worship the Father in spirit and in truth... I who speak to you am He" (John 4:23-26).

Jesus openly told her: **He is the Messiah.**

She left her jar behind and ran into town.

She told everyone what had happened.

And because of her testimony, many Samaritans believed in Him.

This wasn't just a personal encounter.

It was a moment of revelation — and it changed a whole community.

Takeaway: You Are Fully Known and Fully Loved

Jesus didn't wait for the woman at the well to clean up her past or fix her mistakes.

He met her right where she was — carrying shame, hiding pain, and feeling unworthy.

And still, He offered her living water.

Still, He spoke to her with kindness.

Still, He called her seen, known, and loved.

That same love is for you.

You don't have to hide your past.

You don't have to pretend everything is perfect.

Reflection Questions

- Have you ever felt like you had to hide certain parts of yourself — your thoughts, struggles, or past — from God or others? Why?

- How would your life change if you truly believed that Jesus already sees every part of you and loves you just as you are?

Prayer

Jesus,

Thank You for loving me fully, even when I feel unworthy.

Thank You for seeing every part of me and still calling me Your own.

Help me live in the freedom of Your love, without hiding or fear.

Teach me to love others the same way You love me.

Amen.

Faith Challenge

Take a few quiet minutes today.

Talk honestly with Jesus about something you usually try to hide — a fear, a mistake, a worry.

Then remind yourself:

"Jesus sees it all. And He loves me completely."

Let His love wash away your shame.

Chapter 29: The Good Samaritan — Loving People Who Are Different

Have you ever seen someone hurting and wondered if you should help? Maybe you wanted to, but you felt too busy.

Maybe you were scared to get involved. Maybe you weren't sure if they were "your kind of person."

It's easy to care about people who look like us, talk like us, or believe the same things we do. It's harder to love people who are different. But Jesus teaches us that real love crosses every line.

The Bible Story (Luke 10:25-37, Retold)

One day, a religious expert asked Jesus a big question: "What must I do to inherit eternal life?"

Jesus answered, "Love God with all your heart, soul, strength, and mind — and love your neighbor as yourself."

The expert, trying to justify himself, asked, "And who is my neighbor?"

So Jesus told a story. A man was traveling down a dangerous road when he was attacked by robbers. They beat him, stole everything he had, and left him half-dead on the side of the road. A priest — someone who worked in the temple — came walking by.

He saw the man. But instead of helping, he crossed to the other side of the road and kept walking.

Later, another religious man, a Levite, came by. He also saw the hurting man. And he too crossed to the other side and walked away.

Finally, a Samaritan came by.

Now, Jews and Samaritans didn't get along. They avoided each other whenever they could. But when the Samaritan saw the man lying there, he didn't think about the differences between them.

He didn't wonder if the man was worth helping. He felt compassion. He went to him.

He bandaged his wounds. He put him on his donkey. He took him to an inn and paid for him to be cared for.

Jesus asked, "Who was a neighbor to the man?"

The answer was clear: the one who showed mercy.

Jesus said,

"Go and do the same." (Luke 10:37)

Takeaway: What This Story Teaches Us

The Samaritan in the story crossed every barrier: cultural, religious, personal. He showed compassion when others walked by.

But this parable isn't just about being brave or doing more. It's about seeing that **we are the ones on the side of the road** — wounded, helpless, and in need of rescue.

And Christ is the One who stops for us. Jesus is the true Good Samaritan —

the One who shows mercy when we deserve judgment, who pays the cost to bring us healing, and who calls us to love others with the love we've received.

Real love doesn't come from trying harder. It flows from grace.

We love because He first loved us. Not to earn anything but to reflect the mercy we've already been given.

Reflection Questions

- Have you ever seen someone hurting, excluded, or struggling — but felt unsure if you should get involved? What held you back?
- Is there someone in your world who's different from you — maybe in background, beliefs, or personality — that God might be nudging you to love or serve this week?

Prayer

Jesus,

Thank You for loving me, even when I didn't deserve it.

Help me love others the same way.

Open my eyes to see people who need kindness.

Give me courage to cross lines and reach out with real compassion.

Make my heart more like Yours.

Amen.

Faith Challenge

Look around your school, your neighborhood, or your church this week.

Find someone who might feel alone, different, or overlooked.

Do one small act of kindness for them — a smile, a kind word, sitting with them, inviting them in.

Real love is seen in real actions.

Chapter 30: Mary and Martha — Choosing What Matters Most

Do you ever feel like there's just too much to do? Homework. Chores. Friends. Notifications.

Sometimes even good things can leave you feeling rushed and distracted. That's exactly how Martha felt when Jesus came to visit.

She was trying to do everything right. But her sister Mary chose something different.

And Jesus gently showed Martha, and us, what truly matters most.

The Bible Story (Luke 10:38–42, Retold)

Jesus came to the village of Bethany. He was welcomed into the home of two sisters — Mary and Martha.

Martha went straight to work. She was cooking, cleaning, and trying to make everything perfect for Jesus.

Mary, on the other hand, sat down at Jesus's feet and just listened. Martha was frustrated.

She came to Jesus and said, **"Lord, don't You care that my sister has left me to do all the work by myself? Tell her to help me!"**

But Jesus answered kindly:

"Martha, Martha... you are worried and upset about many things, but only one thing is truly needed. Mary has chosen what is better, and it won't be taken away from her."

Jesus wasn't saying that serving is bad. He loved Martha.

But He wanted her to see that her value didn't come from doing everything —

it came from being with Him.

Takeaway Lesson: You Don't Have to Do More to Be Loved

It's easy to believe the lie that being busy equals being important. That we have to keep doing more, achieving more, proving ourselves — just to be enough.

But Jesus invites us into something better:

rest, presence, and love that's already ours.

Martha was doing good things. She was serving, planning, making everything just right.

But in all the doing, she almost missed what mattered most: **being with Jesus.**

Mary wasn't lazy. She was intentional. She chose to sit, listen, and soak in every word from the One who loved her most.

Jesus didn't correct Martha because her work was bad. He corrected her because her **heart was distracted.**

Sometimes, the most powerful thing you can do is stop. Not to be unproductive, but to be **present.**

Jesus wants more than your checklist. He wants your attention. He wants your heart.

Reflection Questions

- Do you feel more like Mary or Martha in this season of your life — and why?

- What's one thing that tends to distract you from simply being still with Jesus?

- What would it look like this week to press pause and choose time with God over pressure to keep performing?

(You don't need to earn God's love. You just need to come close — and sit for a while.)

Prayer

Jesus,

I'm often like Martha — busy, worried, and distracted.

But I want to be like Mary — present, listening, and still.

Help me remember that You love me, even when I stop doing and just sit with You.

Teach me what really matters most.

Amen.

Faith Challenge

Pick one day this week to spend 10 distraction-free minutes with Jesus.

No phone. No to-do list.

Just sit, be still, and listen.

Read a short Scripture.

Then pray:

"Jesus, I'm here. I want to choose You today."

Chapter 31: Jesus and the Adulterous Woman — Grace Instead of Shame

Have you ever felt like your mistake defined you? Like people only saw what you did wrong — not who you really are?

Shame can make you want to hide, run, or give up. But when Jesus meets a woman caught in sin and surrounded by judgment, He responds in a way no one expected.

He doesn't throw stones.

He offers grace.

The Bible Story (John 8:1-11, Retold)

It was morning, and Jesus was teaching in the temple courts. A crowd gathered to hear Him.

Suddenly, a group of religious leaders pushed through the people, dragging a woman with them.

They threw her in the center. "Teacher," they said, "This woman was caught in the act of adultery. The law says we should stone her. What do You say?"

They weren't really asking because they cared about justice — they were trying to trap Jesus.

Jesus didn't answer.

He bent down and wrote something in the dust with His finger. The crowd waited.

Finally, He stood up and said, **"Let the one who has never sinned throw the first stone."**

Silence.

Then — one by one — people started to leave.

Until it was just Jesus and the woman. He looked at her and said, **"Where are your accusers? Has no one condemned you?"**

"No one, Lord," she said.

"Then neither do I. Go now and leave your life of sin."

Jesus didn't ignore her sin. But He didn't shame her.

He offered her something she never expected: grace.

Takeaway: Jesus Doesn't Cancel — He Restores

In a world that's quick to cancel and slow to forgive,

Jesus offers something radical: **grace.**

The woman in this story stood in front of a crowd ready to condemn her.

Everyone saw her failure.

Everyone wanted to define her by her worst mistake.

But Jesus didn't.

He didn't excuse the sin.

But He also didn't throw a stone.

He extended **mercy.**

He gave her dignity.

He offered a new beginning.

The truth is, we've all messed up.

We've all carried shame or regret.

But with Jesus, **shame is never the end.**

You are not the sum of your failures.

You are not trapped in your past.

Jesus doesn't define you by what you've done —

He defines you by **who you are to Him**: loved, seen, and worth restoring.

When others walk away, He leans in.

When you expect judgment, He offers healing.

Jesus doesn't cancel your story.

He rewrites it with grace.

Reflection Questions

- Have you ever felt ashamed of something you've done — something you hoped no one would ever find out?

- How would it change your view of yourself if you imagined Jesus standing with you and saying, "I don't condemn you"?

- Is there someone in your life — a friend, a classmate, even yourself — who needs grace instead of judgment?

(Grace is powerful. It heals, it frees, and it rewrites stories — including yours.)

Prayer

Jesus,

Sometimes I feel like that woman —

exposed, afraid, and unsure if I deserve forgiveness.

But You don't reject me.

You speak love over my shame.

Help me believe that Your grace is bigger than my guilt.

Teach me to offer that grace to others too.

Amen.

Faith Challenge

If you're carrying something heavy from your past,

take a moment today to lay it down.

Write it on a piece of paper.

Then tear it up — and throw it away.

Say aloud:

"Jesus, You forgive me. I don't have to carry this anymore."

Then walk forward in freedom.

Chapter 32: Zacchaeus — Seen and Changed by Love

Have you ever felt invisible? Maybe you've walked into a room and felt like no one even noticed you were there.

Or maybe you felt noticed — but only for your mistakes.

Zacchaeus knew exactly what that felt like. But Jesus shows us that no matter who you are or what you've done, **you are seen, known, and loved.**

The Bible Story (Luke 19:1–10, Retold)

Zacchaeus wasn't a popular guy. He was a tax collector — and not just any tax collector, but a chief one.

Tax collectors back then were known for being cheaters and thieves, taking extra money from people and keeping it for themselves.

Most people hated Zacchaeus.

They saw him as a bad person, a traitor, someone who could never change. One day, Zacchaeus heard that Jesus was coming to town.

He wanted to see Him, but Zacchaeus had a problem: he was very short. The crowds were so big that Zacchaeus couldn't even get a glimpse of Jesus.

So, he did something unexpected: he climbed up into a sycamore tree. From up high, he could finally see over the crowd.

As Jesus walked by, something amazing happened. Jesus stopped, looked up at the tree, and said: **"Zacchaeus, come down immediately. I must stay at your house today."** (Luke 19:5)

Imagine how shocked Zacchaeus must have been. Everyone else saw him as a cheat and a thief. But Jesus saw him as someone worth stopping for.

Zacchaeus climbed down quickly and joyfully welcomed Jesus.

The crowd grumbled: *"Why is Jesus spending time with a sinner?"*

But Zacchaeus's heart was already changing.

He said:

"I will give half of my possessions to the poor, and if I've cheated anyone, I'll pay back four times the amount!"

Jesus smiled and said:

"Today, salvation has come to this house."

Takeaway: God Sees Beyond Your Past

To the crowd, Zacchaeus was a traitor. A thief. A man defined by greed and betrayal. They saw his sin — and they weren't wrong.

But Jesus saw more than just what he had done. He saw someone lost... and someone worth saving.

Jesus didn't demand perfection first. But He didn't ignore sin either.

He called Zacchaeus by name, invited Himself in, and brought a grace that led to transformation. Zacchaeus didn't just feel noticed. He was changed. He repented.

He gave back what he had stolen.

Because encountering Jesus doesn't just lift shame, it leads to a new life.

You may feel like your past defines you. Like your mistakes have already written your story.

But Jesus came for people exactly like Zacchaeus, and like you.

Your value isn't based on your record or reputation.

It's rooted in the mercy of God who made you and the righteousness of Christ offered to you.

And when you respond to that call — like Zacchaeus did — everything can change.

Reflection Questions

- Have you ever felt like your past or reputation made it hard for others to truly see you — or for you to forgive yourself?
- How does it make you feel to know that Jesus sees everything about you — and still loves you fully, without hesitation?
- What might change in your life if you believed Jesus wanted to "come over" — to walk with you, just as you are?

(He's not waiting for you to get it all together. He's just waiting for your "yes.")

Prayer

Jesus,

Thank You for seeing me, knowing me, and loving me even when others don't.

Thank You that I am not stuck in my past.

Help me respond to Your love with a heart that is ready to change.

Teach me to see others with the same grace and hope that You see me.

Amen.

Faith Challenge

This week, do something that shows love to someone others often overlook — a kid sitting alone, a person others ignore, or someone who feels invisible.

Be the person who notices, just like Jesus did.

Chapter 33: The Lost Son — Always Welcome Home

Have you ever made a choice you regretted? Maybe you thought you knew best or you pushed away the people who cared about you.

Jesus told a story about a son who made huge mistakes — but found out something amazing: **No matter how far you run, God's arms are always open.**

The Bible Story (Luke 15:11-32, Retold)

Jesus once told a short story to teach a deep truth.

There was a man who had two sons. One day, the younger son went to his father and said, *"I want my inheritance now."*

In their culture, asking for your inheritance early was like saying, *"I wish you were dead."*

But the father agreed.

He divided his property and gave the younger son his share. The son packed up everything and moved far away. He spent all the money quickly on wild living, parties, and bad choices.

Then a famine hit. The son had no money, friends or food left.

He got a job feeding pigs — a dirty, disgusting job for someone from his background. He was so hungry, he wished he could eat the pigs' food.

Finally, he realized how far he had fallen. He decided to go back home, but he didn't expect to be welcomed as a son. He hoped maybe he could work as a servant.

As he got close to home, his father saw him and ran to him. He threw his arms around his son, and kissed him.

The son started to apologize, *"I don't deserve to be your son..."*

But the father interrupted.

He called for the best robe, a ring, new sandals. He threw a giant party. He said:

"This son of mine was dead and is alive again; he was lost and is found." (Luke 15:24)

The father never stopped loving him.

Not for one second.

The older brother wasn't happy when his brother was being celebrated while he himself had stayed home, worked hard, and followed the rules.

But his father gently reminded him: "You are always with me, and everything I have is yours. But we had to celebrate because your brother was lost and now he's found."

This story reminds us that God's love isn't earned. It's offered — freely, fully, and for everyone who turns to Him.

Takeaway: God's Love Never Runs Out

In Jesus' story, the son didn't come home proudly. He came home humbled, repentant, and aware of what he had done wrong.

But, his father didn't meet him with punishment. Instead, he showed compassion because his son had returned home with a changed heart — and the father was eager to forgive.

That's how God responds to us. He calls you to turn — to come home honestly, to repent, and receive the grace only He can give.

Reflection Questions

- Have you ever felt like you messed up too badly — like maybe you'd disappointed God or couldn't return to Him? What made you feel that way?

- How does it feel to imagine God running toward you, not to punish you, but to hug you and call you His child?

- What's one step you could take this week to return to God — whether it's through prayer, honesty, or simply saying "I'm back"?

(You don't have to earn your way home. Just come — He's already waiting with love.)

Prayer

God,

Sometimes I run away, thinking I know better.

Sometimes I make choices that leave me feeling lost and ashamed.

Thank You for always loving me.

Thank You for welcoming me back with open arms.

Teach me to trust Your mercy and live in Your love.

Amen.

Faith Challenge

If there's something you've been hiding from God — a mistake, a secret, a fear — talk to Him about it today.

Remember:

You don't have to clean yourself up to come home.

You just have to come.

God's arms are already open.

Chapter 34: Jesus Washes the Disciples' Feet — Serving with Love

Have you ever thought that being great means being served by others? Maybe you've seen people act like they're "too important" to do the small, messy things.

But Jesus showed something totally different: **Real greatness comes from serving others with love.**

The Bible Story (John 13:1-17, Retold)

Theis story begins the night before Jesus would be arrested and crucified.

He knew His time with His disciples was almost over. Every word and action carried weight.

Before dinner, something surprising happened. In those days, people walked everywhere — through dust, dirt, and animal-filled streets. By the time they arrived for a meal, their feet were filthy.

It was normal for a servant to wash guests' feet. But that night, no one had done it.

Then, Jesus, their Lord, their Teacher, the Son of God, got up. He removed His outer robe. He tied a towel around His waist. He poured water into a basin. And one by one, He knelt to wash His disciples' feet.

Even Judas.

Jesus knew Judas would betray Him. And still... He knelt before him. He served him.

It stunned the room.

Peter even tried to stop Him. But Jesus told him this had to happen. When He finished, Jesus said: "Now that I, your Lord and Teacher, have washed your feet, you also should wash one another's feet." (John 13:14)

He wasn't just giving them a lesson in hygiene. He was giving them a picture of the Kingdom.

Real leadership looks like humility. Real love looks like service, even when it's uncomfortable or undeserved.

Jesus showed them what it means to love with no strings attached. Then He told them:

Go and do the same.

Takeaway: True Greatness Looks Like Serving

When Jesus knelt to wash His disciples' feet, it was a glimpse of the cross. A picture of how He would humble Himself even further — giving His life to cleanse us from sin.

His act of humility pointed to something far deeper: We don't just need an example — we need a Savior.

But once we've received His grace, He calls us to reflect it, to love boldly.

True greatness isn't about being seen, it's about surrender.

When you serve others you're truly walking in the way of your Savior, who knelt low to lift us up.

Reflection Questions

- Have you ever had a moment where you served someone even though it was difficult, unnoticed, or inconvenient? What was that like?

- What's one small way you can serve someone this week — at home, school, or church — with quiet strength and love?

- What would it look like to lead by lowering yourself, just like Jesus did?

(Greatness in God's Kingdom begins with a towel, not a throne.)

Prayer

Jesus,

Thank You for showing me what true love looks like.

Thank You for not acting too important to serve others.

Teach me to be humble.

Teach me to love people the way You do — not just with words, but with actions.

Help me find joy in lifting others up.

Amen.

Faith Challenge

Find one way to serve someone this week —

- Help a friend without being asked.
- Do a chore without seeking praise.
- Write a note of encouragement.
- Pick up after someone else without complaining.

Every small act of service plants seeds of love.

Chapter 35: Crucifixion and Resurrection — Stronger Than Death

The resurrection of Jesus is the moment that changed everything. Jesus died for our sins, and when He rose, it proved that sin was paid for, death was defeated, and Satan had lost.

The resurrection is not the end of a sad story —it's the beginning of a new one, sealed with power, hope, and eternal victory.

The Bible Story (John 19–20, Retold)

Jesus had spent years teaching people about God's love, healing the sick, forgiving sins, and bringing hope to everyone He met. He lived a life full of truth, kindness, and courage.

But not everyone liked what Jesus was doing. The religious leaders felt threatened by Him. They were jealous, afraid, and angry. They plotted to kill Him.

One night, Jesus was arrested. His closest friends ran away, terrified.

He was put on trial, though He had done nothing wrong. The crowd — the same crowd that had once cheered for Him — now shouted, "Crucify Him!"

Jesus was beaten, mocked, and nailed to a wooden cross. He hung there, bleeding, while people jeered and soldiers gambled for His clothes.

Then, in deep pain, Jesus cried out: **"It is finished."** (John 19:30)

He bowed His head and died.

It seemed like the end.

Hope seemed crushed.

His followers hid in fear, broken-hearted.

But it wasn't the end.

Three days later, early in the morning, some women went to Jesus's tomb.

They found the stone rolled away.

The tomb was empty.

An angel told them the incredible news:

"He is not here; He has risen!" (Luke 24:6)

Jesus had defeated death.

He is alive.

Hope wasn't dead — it was stronger than ever.

Takeaway: The Cross Paid It All. The Resurrection Proves It.

Jesus didn't die just to show how much He loves you — He died to take your place. At the cross, He bore the full weight of our sins. He was pierced for our transgressions, and in His death, the debt was paid.

But the story doesn't end at the cross. Three days later, Jesus rose again as a declaration of victory.

His resurrection proves that His sacrifice was accepted. It means sin has been conquered, death has been defeated, and Satan has lost.

Now, for everyone who turns to Him in repentance and faith, there is forgiveness, freedom, and eternal life (Romans 10:9–10).

Jesus is alive — and He is Lord.

Reflection Question

- How does knowing Jesus conquered death itself give you courage to face what you're walking through?

Prayer

Jesus,

Thank You for loving me enough to die for me.

Thank You for rising again and proving that love is stronger than death.

Help me trust in Your victory when life feels hard.

Teach me to live every day with the hope and courage You give.

Amen.

Faith Challenge

Take a moment today to write down something you feel is "over" or "too broken."

Then, next to it, write this:

"Nothing is impossible with God." (Luke 1:37)

Pray over it.

Ask Jesus to bring new life where you feel stuck or hopeless.

Resurrection isn't just something that happened long ago — it's a power that still changes lives today.

Chapter 36: The Thief on the Cross — It's Never Too Late

Have you ever felt like you missed your chance? Like it's too late to fix what you've done, too late to change, too late for God to still care about you?

The thief on the cross thought his story was over. He had wasted his life and he was dying.

But in his very last moments, he looked to Jesus and discovered that grace still had room for him.

The Bible Story (Luke 23:32-43, Retold)

As Jesus was crucified, two criminals hung on either side of Him. One joined the voices of the crowd, sneering at Jesus: "If You're really the Messiah, save Yourself — and us!"

The other man responded differently. He wasn't just facing death — he was facing truth. He rebuked the first thief: "Don't you fear God? We're getting what we deserve. But this man has done nothing wrong."

In that moment, he saw something the others missed. He recognized Jesus not as a victim, but as a King. Not as a criminal, but as the righteous Judge.

And with nothing to offer — no way to earn grace — he turned to Jesus in faith and said:

"Jesus, remember me when You come into Your kingdom."

It wasn't a last-minute escape. It was a humble confession. A plea of repentance. A cry for mercy.

Jesus answered with a promise that reached beyond death: "Truly I tell you, today you will be with Me in paradise." No religious performance. No ability to fix his past. Just a repentant heart, real faith, and a Savior full of grace.

Takeaway: It's Never Too Late for Grace

God's grace isn't earned by good behavior or a perfect track record. It's offered through faith in Jesus, even at the final breath.

The thief on the cross couldn't go back and fix his past. He couldn't make up for the wrong he'd done. But in a moment of clarity, he saw who Jesus really was: The Savior, the Son of God.

In that moment, he turned to Christ in faith and repentance, trusting Him as Lord.

Jesus responded with a promise: "Today, you will be with Me in paradise."

This is a picture of what real saving faith looks like — a heart that confesses guilt, recognizes Jesus as King, and asks for mercy.

If you turn to Jesus with a repentant heart and trust Him fully, His answer will be the same: Welcome home.

Reflection Questions

- Have you ever felt like it was too late to turn your life around or get close to God again? What made you feel that way?

- What does the story of the thief on the cross reveal about Jesus's heart — especially for people who feel like they've failed?

- What would it look like for you to trust Jesus with **your whole story** — even the messy, broken, or unfinished parts?

(Grace isn't earned. It's received — and it's always waiting for you to say yes.)

Prayer

Jesus,

Sometimes I feel like I've missed my chance.

Like I've failed too much or waited too long.

But Your words to the thief give me hope.

You never give up on us.

Help me trust that it's not too late for me.

I believe You remember me — and that Your grace is enough.

Amen.

Faith Challenge

Write this as a reminder and place it where you'll see it:

"God still calls sinners to repent — but the time to answer is now."

Do not wait. Grace is real, but it is not endless on your terms. "Now is the day of salvation" (2 Corinthians 6:2). You are not beyond reach, but you are not promised another hour (Hebrews 9:27). Respond while the door   is   open.

Chapter 37: Thomas Doubts — When You Need Proof

Have you ever had questions about God? Like, "Is this even real?" Or, "Why doesn't He just show me something clear?"

You're not the only one.

One of Jesus's own disciples — Thomas — wrestled with serious doubt. But Jesus met him with grace.

The Bible Story (John 20:24-29, Retold)

It was just days after Jesus had risen from the dead. The disciples were gathered together — excited, confused, amazed. They had seen Jesus alive again.

But Thomas wasn't there. When the others told him, "We've seen the Lord!" he just couldn't believe it.

"Unless I see the nail marks in His hands," Thomas said, "and put my finger where the nails were... I won't believe it."

He wasn't being difficult. He just needed proof.

A week later, the disciples were together again. This time, Thomas was there. And suddenly, Jesus appeared. Right in the room with them.

He looked at Thomas and said, **"Put your finger here. See My hands. Reach out your hand and put it into My side. Stop doubting and believe."**

Thomas fell to his knees and said, **"My Lord and my God!"**

Jesus replied, **"You believe because you've seen Me.**

Blessed are those who haven't seen — and still believe."

Takeaway: Doubt Isn't the End of Faith

Thomas wanted to know that it was real.

He had seen pain, loss, and confusion. He wasn't ready to believe without something he could touch, see, and understand.

Instead of scolding him, **Jesus met him in his doubt.** He offered His hands. He invited Thomas closer. That's grace.

Doubt doesn't disqualify you. It doesn't mean you're a bad Christian. It means you're **wrestling honestly** with big questions — and that's part of real faith.

What matters is that you bring your questions to Jesus. Don't hide them. Don't carry them alone.

Jesus wants to walk with you through your doubts. He'll lead you to something deeper, stronger, and more personal than blind belief. He offers proof, presence, and peace.

Reflection Questions

- Have you ever had doubts about your faith — about God's existence, His goodness, or whether He's really listening? What was that like?

- If you could ask Jesus one honest question today, what would it be?

- How does it feel to know that Jesus didn't shame Thomas — He welcomed him with kindness and gave him exactly what he needed?

(Faith doesn't mean you never doubt. It means you bring your doubt to the One who understands — and stays.)

Prayer

Jesus,

Sometimes I wrestle with doubts.

I want to believe, but I also want proof.

Thank You for not pushing Thomas away — and for not pushing me away either.

Help me keep seeking You.

Help me believe, even when it's hard.

Amen.

Faith Challenge

Take five minutes to write out your honest questions for God.

Don't hold back — He already knows your heart.

Then pray this simple line:

"Jesus, show me who You really are."

Look for ways He might answer — in Scripture, in quiet moments, or through others.

Chapter 38: Peter Is Restored — When You've Messed Up Big

Have you ever made a mistake that you thought couldn't be fixed?

That's how Peter felt. He didn't just mess up a little. He denied even knowing Jesus... three times.

But after the worst moment of his life, something beautiful happened. Jesus came back for him.

The Bible Story (John 21:1–19, Retold)

Peter had once told Jesus, "I'll never leave You."

But on the night Jesus was arrested, Peter was scared. Three different people asked if he was one of Jesus's followers. And all three times, he said no.

"I don't know Him."

And then — the rooster crowed. Just like Jesus said it would.

Peter realized what he'd done. He ran away and wept bitterly. Days later, after Jesus had risen from the dead,

Peter and some of the other disciples went back to fishing. One morning, they saw someone on the shore calling out to them.

It was Jesus.

When Peter realized who it was, he jumped into the water and swam to shore. Jesus had made breakfast. After they ate, Jesus looked at Peter and asked, **"Do you love Me?"**

Peter said, "Yes, Lord. You know I do." Jesus asked again. And again.

Three times — just like the three times Peter had denied Him. But this time, Jesus wasn't shaming Peter. He was restoring him.

And then He said,

"Feed My sheep."

"Follow Me."

Jesus was saying:

I still believe in you.

I still want you.

Let's start again.

Takeaway: God Doesn't Give Up on You

Peter didn't just make a small mistake — he denied even knowing Jesus.

Three times.

At the very moment Jesus needed him most. And yet...

Jesus didn't write Peter off. He didn't hold it over his head. **He came back to restore him.**

That's what Jesus does. He sees your worst moment, and still chooses you. Not to shame you, but to **rewrite your story.**

He looks for hearts willing to return.

Peter's failure didn't end his story — it shaped it. Through grace, he became one of the boldest leaders the Church has ever known.

So, remember:

You are not disqualified.

You are not too broken.

You are not your failure.

Jesus still calls your name.

And He still believes in you.

Reflection Questions

- Have you ever felt like you made a mistake too big to come back from — something that made you feel ashamed or unworthy?

- What would it mean to truly believe that Jesus sees your failure and still says, "I'm not done with you"?

- What's one step you can take today to walk forward in grace, not guilt?

(Jesus doesn't give up on you — and He's still writing your story.)

Prayer

> *Jesus,*
>
> *I've made mistakes.*
>
> *I've said things and done things I regret.*
>
> *But You didn't give up on Peter — and I believe You won't give up on me.*
>
> *Help me receive Your forgiveness,*
>
> *and follow You with a whole heart.*
>
> *Amen.*

Faith Challenge

Take time today to write a letter — from Jesus to you.

Start it with:

"I know what you did... and I still love you."

Let those words remind you that your failure is not the end of your story.

Section 5: Faith That Changes the World (Acts – Revelation)

Jesus rose from the dead, but that wasn't the end of the story. It was just the beginning. In this section, you'll meet bold believers like Stephen, Philip, and Paul who carried the message of Jesus into the world. You'll discover the power God gives us to stand strong, speak truth, and share our faith. And you'll see how the story ends, not in fear, but in a future filled with hope. This is what happens when faith moves from your heart to your life: it doesn't just change you: it starts changing the world.

Chapter 39: Stephen Stands Strong — Faith That Speaks Boldly

Have you ever been afraid to speak up for what you believe? Being bold about your faith isn't easy, especially when people push back.

But Stephen was one of the first followers of Jesus who showed what true courage looks like. Even when it cost him everything, he stood strong because he knew who he stood for.

The Bible Story (Acts 6–7, Retold)

Stephen was one of the early believers in the church. He wasn't one of the twelve apostles — he was chosen to help serve the community, especially the widows and the poor.

But Stephen wasn't just a helper. He was full of the Holy Spirit. He spoke with wisdom, power, and love.

Some religious leaders didn't like that. They argued with him but they couldn't outsmart him. So, they spread lies. They said he was speaking against God.

They dragged him in front of a council and accused him. Even then, Stephen didn't back down. He stood up and told the truth about how the people had ignored God's voice and rejected Jesus, the Son of God.

It made the leaders furious. They rushed at him, dragged him outside the city, and began to stone him.

But as Stephen was dying, he looked up and saw something incredible: Jesus, standing at the right hand of God, watching him.

And Stephen prayed,

"Lord, don't hold this sin against them."

Just like Jesus, he forgave, even in the middle of pain.

Takeaway: Real Faith Remains — Even When It Costs Everything

Stephen's story is powerful and sobering. He didn't just believe quietly; he spoke boldly about Jesus, even when the crowd turned violent. He was falsely accused, dragged out of the city, and stoned to death. But through it all, he didn't respond with hate. He looked to heaven, forgave his enemies, and trusted Jesus until his final breath. Stephen reminds us that following Jesus is not about popularity or safety. It's about truth, courage, and eternal hope. When you take a stand for Christ, it may not be easy — but you're never alone. Jesus stood for Stephen in heaven (Acts 7:55–56), and He stands with you now. Faith that endures, even through rejection or suffering, points to a Savior who's worth everything.

Reflection Questions

- Have you ever had a moment where you stayed quiet about your faith because you were afraid of what others might think or say? How did that feel?

- What do you think gave Stephen the strength to stay faithful even when everything seemed to be against him?

- What's one specific way you could live or speak boldly for Jesus this week — with kindness, clarity, and love?

(You're not alone when you stand for Jesus. He's standing with you — and that changes everything.)

Prayer

Jesus,

I want to have faith like Stephen.

A faith that stands when it's scary.

A voice that speaks truth with love.

Give me courage, not to impress others,

but to honor You.

Stand with me — and help me stand for You.

Amen.

Faith Challenge

Think of one situation this week where you could speak kindly and clearly about your faith —

maybe in a conversation with a friend,

a social media post,

or standing up for someone who's left out.

Ask God for boldness.

Then do it — with love.

Chapter 40: Pentecost — The Power to Change the World

Have you ever felt too small to make a difference? It's easy to think you have to wait until you're older, smarter, or stronger to matter.

But the story of Pentecost shows that when God's Spirit fills you, you have everything you need to live boldly right now.

The Bible Story (Acts 2, Retold)

After Jesus rose from the dead, He spent time with His followers. He taught them more about God's Kingdom and gave them a mission: "Go and tell the whole world about Me."

But Jesus also knew they would need help to do it. So before He returned to heaven, He made a promise: **"You will receive power when the Holy Spirit comes on you; and you will be my witnesses."** (Acts 1:8)

The followers of Jesus gathered together in a room, waiting for this promise. They didn't know exactly what to expect. They just trusted. Then, on the day of Pentecost, it happened.

Suddenly, a sound like a rushing wind filled the room. Flames of fire appeared and rested on each person's head but no one was burned. All of them were filled with the Holy Spirit.

They began speaking in different languages, so that people from all over the world could hear the message of Jesus in their own words.

Crowds gathered, amazed and confused.

Peter, one of Jesus's closest friends, stood up and boldly preached about Jesus — the same Peter who had once been too scared to even admit he knew Him.

Thousands of people believed that day. The Church was born.

Ordinary people, filled with God's Spirit, began changing the world.

Takeaway: God's Power Has a Purpose

The power of the Holy Spirit is about making Jesus known. At Pentecost, God poured out His Spirit to launch a movement that would reach the ends of the earth. Peter stood up, not to promote himself, but to proclaim Christ crucified and risen. When the people asked, "What should we do?" the answer was clear: "Repent and be baptized in the name of Jesus Christ for the forgiveness of your sins" (Acts 2:38). That's where the Spirit leads us — not to self-promotion, but to surrender. If you've trusted in Jesus, the same Spirit now lives in you. He gives courage to share the gospel, strength to live differently, and boldness to stand for truth. You weren't filled just to feel powerful. You were filled to carry the good news. Because God's mission isn't finished. And He invites you to be part of it.

Reflection Questions

- What's one way you want to make a difference for God — at school, in your friendships, or in your community?

- How does it change the way you see yourself when you remember that the Holy Spirit lives inside of you — right now, not just someday?

- What's one area of your life where you want to rely more on the Holy Spirit's help this week?

(God didn't just call you — He equipped you. His Spirit is your power, your guide, and your strength.)

Prayer

Holy Spirit,

Thank You for living inside me.

Help me remember that with Your power, I can face anything and share Your love boldly.

Fill me with courage when I feel afraid.

Use my life to bring hope, truth, and love to the world around me.

Amen.

Faith Challenge

Today, ask God for one opportunity to show His love or speak His truth.

It could be encouraging someone who feels forgotten.

It could be standing up for what's right.

It could be sharing your story.

You are not waiting to be important.

You are filled with God's power right now.

Chapter 41: Paul's Story — God Can Use Anyone

Have you ever felt like your past disqualifies you from doing something good? Maybe you think, *"God can use other people... but not someone like me."*

But God doesn't wait for perfect people. He changes people — and then uses their story to change the world. That's what happened with Paul.

The Bible Story (Acts 9, Retold)

Before Paul was known as one of the greatest missionaries and writers in the Bible, his name was Saul. Hel was known for something else: hunting down Christians.

He believed that followers of Jesus were dangerous. He arrested them. He approved of violence against them. He was feared.

But God had a different plan for Saul's life.

One day, Saul was traveling to a city called Damascus to arrest more Christians. On the way, a bright light flashed from heaven.

He fell to the ground and heard a voice: **"Saul, Saul, why are you persecuting Me?"** (Acts 9:4) It was Jesus.

Saul was stunned. Blinded by the light, he couldn't see for three days. But during that time, everything inside him began to change.

God sent a man named Ananias to pray for him. When Ananias placed his hands on Saul, his sight returned, and his heart was never the same.

Saul became Paul: a new man with a new mission.

Instead of destroying the Church, he began building it. He traveled, preached, wrote letters, and helped people discover the same grace he had found.

God used Paul — with all his failures, all his past, all his brokenness — to spread the Gospel across the world.

Takeaway: God Uses Broken People to Do Big Things

If you've ever believed the lie that your past disqualifies you, look at Paul.

Before he followed Jesus, Paul was the last person anyone would expect God to use. He had a bad history, but God didn't see a lost cause.

He saw a future.

God stepped in with grace and purpose and changed the course of Paul's life.

Always remember: God isn't looking for perfection. He's looking for willing hearts. He takes your broken pieces and builds something powerful.

When you give your whole story — the good, the bad, the scarred — to Jesus, nothing is wasted.

God can redeem anything. And He can use you — right now, right where you are — for something bigger than you imagine.

God didn't just forgive Paul — He sent him. Paul became a bold missionary, church planter, and writer of much of the New Testament. God used Paul's voice to spread the gospel to new nations and generations. The same God who called Paul has a purpose for your life, too — and when you follow His lead, your story can echo far beyond what you see.

Reflection Questions

- What part of your past makes it hard for you to believe God could use you — a mistake, a regret, a label?

- What would it look like to give that specific part of your story to God and trust Him to use it for something good?

- Who in your life might need to hear how God has been working through your journey?

(You don't have to be perfect. You just have to be willing. God writes beauty out of broken stories — including yours.)

Prayer

God,

Sometimes I feel like I'm too messed up to be used by You.

But I see in Paul's life that You take broken people and do amazing things through them.

Take all of me — the good, the bad, the hurt, the hope — and use it for Your glory.

Thank You for loving me as I am and never giving up on me.

Amen.

Faith Challenge

Write down one part of your story you've tried to hide or run from — something that's brought guilt or shame.

Then pray this:

"God, this is Yours now. Use it however You want."

Let go of the weight of your past.

Your story is not too messy.

God can use it to bring light into someone else's darkness.

Chapter 42: Philip and the Ethiopian — Sharing Your Faith Naturally

Have you ever wanted to talk about your faith, but didn't know how to start? The story of Philip and the Ethiopian shows us something powerful: Sharing your faith doesn't have to be forced. It can happen naturally through listening, caring, and simply being open when the moment comes.

The Bible Story (Acts 8:26–40, Retold)

Philip was a follower of Jesus and part of the early church. One day, an angel gave him very clear instructions: "Go south, to the desert road that leads from Jerusalem to Gaza." Philip obeyed.

As he walked, he saw a man in a chariot: an Ethiopian official, important and intelligent. He had just come from Jerusalem and was reading a scroll of Scripture.

The Holy Spirit whispered to Philip, **"Go to that chariot and stay near it."**

Philip ran up and heard the man reading from the book of Isaiah, a prophecy about the Messiah. Philip asked him, **"Do you understand what you're reading?"**

The man replied, **"How can I, unless someone explains it to me?"**

He invited Philip to sit with him. From there, Philip started with the Scripture the man was reading and told him the Good News about Jesus.

As they traveled together, they came to some water. The man said, "Look! There's water! What's stopping me from being baptized?"

Right there, in the middle of the road, Philip baptized him. Then the Spirit took Philip away, and the man continued on his journey, filled with joy.

Takeaway: You Don't Have to Force It

Philip didn't preach at the Ethiopian man. He simply **showed up**, listened, and responded with love and clarity.

He followed a gentle nudge from God and paid attention to someone's curiosity.

He shared the story of Jesus in a way that felt personal. That's what real faith-sharing looks like. No pressure. Just **presence, patience, and openness**.

God will do the heavy lifting, you just have to be available.

Whether you're walking beside a friend, answering a question in class, or praying quietly for someone who's searching, your faith can shine in simple, honest ways.

Faith isn't about convincing. It's about connecting.

Reflection Questions

- Have you ever had someone ask about your faith — or noticed a moment where you could have shared something? How did it feel?

- What are some fears or doubts that make sharing your faith feel hard or awkward?

- Who in your life might need someone to simply **walk beside them**, listen without judgment, and gently point them toward hope?

(You don't have to force the moment. Just be faithful with it — God will take care of the rest.)

Prayer

God,

Sometimes I feel nervous about sharing my faith.

But I want to be like Philip — open, ready, and willing to follow Your lead.

Help me notice the people around me.

Give me the courage to speak, the humility to listen, and the heart to love others like You do.

Amen.

Faith Challenge

Ask God this simple question today:

"Who do You want me to walk with?"

It might be a friend, a classmate, or someone at home.

Look for one moment to share something real — a prayer, a Bible verse, or just your story.

Let it be natural.

Let it be love.

Let God do the rest.

Chapter 43: Armor of God — Protection for Tough Days

Have you ever felt like life is a battle? Maybe it's a fight to stay strong when you're tired. A fight to hold onto your faith when things go wrong.

You are in a battle — not against people, but against fear, doubt, lies, and discouragement.

The good news is: God gives you everything you need to stand strong.

The Bible Story (Ephesians 6:10-18, Retold)

Paul, the same man whose life was changed by Jesus, wrote a letter to believers explaining how to survive the hard days.

He said, *"Put on the full armor of God, so you can stand against the enemy's attacks."*

Paul wasn't talking about real metal armor. He was talking about spiritual armor , the kind you can't see but need every day.

Here's what he described:

- **Belt of Truth**: Hold onto God's truth, not the lies you hear from the world.

- **Breastplate of Righteousness**: Protect your heart by doing what is right.

- **Shoes of the Gospel of Peace**: Be ready to move and share God's peace wherever you go.

- **Shield of Faith**: Block the fiery arrows of fear, doubt, and temptation.
- **Helmet of Salvation**: Protect your mind by remembering who you are in Christ.
- **Sword of the Spirit**: Fight back with God's Word — the Bible is your weapon.

He reminded them: Pray all the time. Stay alert. Stay strong.

God doesn't leave you defenseless. He arms you with everything you need to stand.

Takeaway: You Are Equipped to Stand Strong

Life is full of battles. But Christ is our strength in our weakness

When you stay close to Jesus and put on His armor every day, you can stand strong no matter what comes against you.

You don't have to fight with anger, fear, or hopelessness. You fight with truth, righteousness, peace, faith, salvation, and the power of God's Word.

You are a warrior in God's army, not because of your strength, but because of His. You are already equipped. Now it's time to put on the armor and live like it.

Reflection Questions

- Which piece of God's armor do you feel you need the most right now?
- What would it look like to put that piece on in your everyday life?

Prayer

God,

Thank You for giving me everything I need to face each day.

Help me to put on Your armor — truth, righteousness, peace, faith, salvation, and Your Word — so I can stand strong against fear, doubt, and lies.

Remind me that I never fight alone.

You are my strength.

Amen.

Faith Challenge

Choose one piece of God's armor today to focus on.

Write it on a sticky note and put it somewhere you'll see it — your mirror, your notebook, your phone.

Every time you see it, remember:

God has already given you the strength you need to stand.

Chapter 44: New Heaven and New Earth — Hope That Never Dies

Have you ever wished for a fresh start? A place with no pain, no sadness, no goodbyes?

Sometimes the world feels so broken that it's hard to believe it could ever really be fixed.

But God promises something incredible: One day, everything broken will be made whole.

Everything wrong will be made right. And the story will end — not in defeat, but in everlasting hope.

The Bible Story (Revelation 21-22, Retold)

Near the end of the Bible, God gave a vision to John, one of Jesus's closest followers. John saw something amazing, something that's still waiting for us in the future.

He saw a new heaven and a new earth. In this new world, God Himself would live with His people. There would be no more death. No more sadness, crying or pain.

John wrote: **"God will wipe every tear from their eyes. There will be no more death or mourning or crying or pain, for the old order of things has passed away."** (Revelation 21:4)

He saw a city shining with beauty, full of light, where God's glory lit everything. He saw a river of life, clear as crystal, flowing from God's throne.

He saw the tree of life, giving fruit that would heal the nations. And he heard God's voice say: **"I am making everything new."** (Revelation 21:5)

This is not a dream. It's a promise.

For everyone who trusts in Jesus, this future is real. It's waiting, and it's better than anything we can imagine.

Takeaway: Your Story Ends in Victory

Right now, life can be hard. But this is not the end.

God has already written the final chapter and it's full of hope. You are part of it.

The promises of God are not just for one day far away. They give you strength today because you know where the story is going.

You are heading toward a forever with God where love wins, life wins, and hope never dies.

Reflection Questions

- What does it mean to you that God promises to wipe away every tear?
- How can believing in God's final victory give you hope for the struggles you're facing today?

Prayer

God,

Thank You for promising a future full of life, love, and hope.

When life feels heavy, remind me that You are making everything new.

Give me the courage to live with joy and trust today because I know my story ends with You.

Thank You for being the God who keeps every promise.

Amen.

Faith Challenge

Whenever life feels too hard or heavy, whisper this to yourself:

"This is not the end. God is making all things new."

Hold onto that hope — because it's true.

Live every day with your eyes on the promise that can never be broken.

Closing Words: Your Journey Is Just Beginning

Faith is a relationship that grows, stretches, and strengthens every day you walk with God.

The stories you have read are about the same God who is still working today in your life, in your choices, in your future.

You will have moments of doubt. You will face giants, storms, and broken roads. You will sometimes wonder if you are strong enough, good enough, or brave enough.

But every step of the way, you will not walk alone.

The same God who called Abraham, strengthened Moses, forgave Peter, and empowered Paul is the same God who calls, strengthens, forgives, and empowers you today.

You do not have to be perfect to walk with God. You only need to trust Him, step by step, day by day, heart to heart.

So, keep going, keep trusting, and keep growing

Your story, written with God's hand, will matter more than you can ever imagine.

Final Prayer

God,

Thank You for leading every reader through this book.

Thank You for writing their lives with love, mercy, and power.

Give them strength when they are tired, hope when they are discouraged, and courage when the road ahead is difficult.

Build their faith deep and wide.

Fill them with Your Spirit and guide their steps.

Use their lives to shine Your truth and love into a world that needs You.

In Jesus' Name, Amen.

Going Deeper — Optional Study Track

Bible Maps — Where It All Happened

Abraham's Journey

- God called Abraham to leave his home and travel to a new land.
- Abraham traveled from **Ur** (in Mesopotamia) to **Haran**, then down into **Canaan** (today's Israel).

Abraham's Journey

From Ur to Haran to Egypt

Mt Ararat

Paddan Aram

Haran

Tigris R

Mediterranean Sea

Damascus
Arabian Desert

Sumer

Egypt

Ur

Red Sea

Moses and the Exodus

- Moses led the Israelites out of slavery in Egypt.
- They crossed the **Red Sea**, traveled through the **Sinai Desert**, and headed toward the **Promised Land**.

Moses' Exodus
From Egypt to Canaan

Egypt

Red Sea

Mount Sinai

Jesus' Ministry Journey

- Jesus traveled through towns like **Bethlehem**, **Nazareth**, **Sea of Galilee**, **Capernaum**, and **Jerusalem**, sharing the Good News.

Jesus' Ministry

Bethlehem

Sea of Galilee

Capernaum

Jerusalem

Paul's Missionary Journeys

- Paul traveled across the Roman world to share Jesus with new believers.
- He visited places like **Antioch, Cyprus, Iconium, Lystra, Ephesus, Philippi, Rome**, and more.

Paul's
MISSIONARY JOURNEYS

Antioch

Cyprus

Lystra

Character Profiles — Real People, Real Faith

The people in the Bible weren't superheroes. They had strengths and weaknesses just like us.

These short profiles will help you see how God used real, imperfect people to do extraordinary things.

Their stories can inspire your own.

- **Strengths:** Brave, worshipful, passionate leader
- **Struggles:** Pride, temptation, big mistakes
- **Why He Matters:** David trusted God when he was young and served Him with a humble heart.

- **Strengths:** Loyal, kind, courageous
- **Struggles:** Loss, loneliness, uncertainty
- **Why She Matters:** Ruth chose to stay faithful to God and to family even when her future looked dark.
- Her loyalty opened doors to blessings she could never have imagined, including becoming part of the family line of Jesus.

- **Strengths:** Courageous, passionate, willing to try
- **Struggles:** Fear, doubt, impulsiveness
- **Why He Matters:** Peter wasn't perfect but Jesus still called him to lead the early church.
- God uses people who fall but get back up in faith.

- **Strengths:** Intelligent, bold, committed
- **Struggles:** Pride, violent past, hardship
- **Why He Matters:** Paul once fought against believers, but after meeting Jesus, he spent his life spreading the Gospel. His story proves that no one is too far gone for God's love.

Key Concepts Explained — Foundations of Your Faith

Some words you hear in church, in the Bible, or from other Christians can sound confusing at first.

Here are three powerful ideas explained simply — because understanding these truths will grow your faith strong.

Grace — God's Gift You Can't Earn

Grace means that **God loves you no matter what** — not because you earned it, not because you deserved it, but because it's who He is.

You can't work for grace.

You can't buy grace.

You can't be "good enough" to get it.

Grace is a free gift.

Jesus offers it to everyone who believes in Him.

"For it is by grace you have been saved, through faith—and this is not from yourselves, it is the gift of God." (Ephesians 2:8)

Covenant — God's Unbreakable Promise

A covenant is **a promise that can't be broken** — even when people fail.

God made covenants with Noah, Abraham, Moses, and others throughout the Bible.

Each time, God promised to love, protect, and guide His people.

When Jesus came, He made a **new covenant:**

Through His sacrifice, anyone who believes can have a forever relationship with God.

"This cup is the new covenant in my blood, which is poured out for you." (Luke 22:20)

Redemption — God Rescues and Restores

Redemption means **buying something back** — rescuing it, restoring it, making it new again.

Jesus redeems us.

Through His death and resurrection, He paid the price to bring us back into God's family.

Redemption is about healing what's broken and giving new life where there was only loss.

"In Him we have redemption through His blood, the forgiveness of sins, in accordance with the riches of God's grace." (Ephesians 1:7)

Memory Verse Challenges — Hide God's Word in Your Heart

Learning Scripture is one of the strongest ways to build your faith.

Even when you do not have a Bible with you, God's truth can live inside you.

When life gets hard, these verses will come back to your heart and give you strength.

Choose your level of challenge:

Faith Builder - Memorize 5 verses

Faith Warrior - Memorize 10 verses

You can track your progress on the page provided below.

MEMORY VERSES TO LEARN

☐ Genesis 1:27: "So God created mankind in his own image, in the image of God he created them; male and female he created them."

☐ Joshua 1:9 "Be strong and courageous. Do not be afraid; do not be discouraged, for the Lord your God will be with you wherever you go."

☐ 1 Samuel 16:7 "The Lord does not look at the things people look at. People look at the outward appearance, but the Lord looks at the heart."

☐ Psalm 46:1
"God is our refuge and strength, an ever-present help in trouble."

☐ Proverbs 3:5-6
"Trust in the Lord with all your heart and lean not on your own understanding; in all your ways submit to him, and he will make your paths straight."

☐ Isaiah 40:31
"But those who hope in the Lord will renew their strength. They will soar on wings like eagles; they will run and not grow weary, they will walk and not be faint."

☐ Matthew 22:37-39
"Love the Lord your God with all your heart and with all your soul and with all your mind... Love your neighbor as yourself."

☐ John 14:6
"Jesus answered, 'I am the way and the truth and the life. No one comes to the Father except through me.'"

☐ Romans 8:28
"And we know that in all things God works for the good of those who love him, who have been called according to his purpose."

☐ Philippians 4:13
"I can do all this through him who gives me strength."

Part 2: The Ultimate Bible Trivia Book for Teens

600 Fun-Filled Questions to Test Your Knowledge, Challenge Friends, and Grow Your Faith

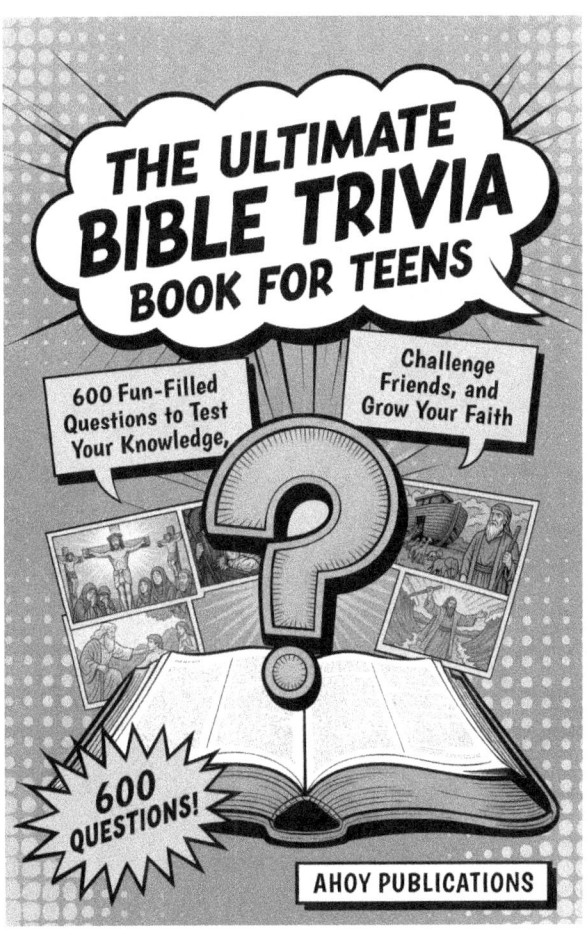

Section 1: Genesis - Revelation

Subsection 1: The Beginning: Way Back When It All Started

Genesis talks about creation, the first people on Earth, and how the stage was set for a Biblical journey. Let's jump right into how it all began.

Multiple Choice Missions:

1. According to the first book of the Bible, what was the first thing God created?

    a) The sun, moon, and stars

    b) Land

    c) Light

    d) Plants and trees

2. What was the name of the special garden where God placed Adam and Eve?

    a) Zion

    b) Eden

    c) Canaan

    d) Galilee

3. There was one tree that God told Adam and Eve not to eat from. Which one was it?

    a) The Tree of Life

    b) The Tree of the Knowledge of Good and Evil

    c) The Tree of Healing

    d) The Tree of Wisdom

4. Who was it that convinced Eve to go against God's command?

    a) An angel

    b) A lion

    c) The serpent

    d) A bird

5. What was the very first thing Adam and Eve realized about themselves right after they ate the forbidden fruit?

    a) They instantly received divine wisdom.

    b) Their eyes were opened, and they realized they were naked.

    c) They could now understand and speak every animal's language.

    d) They were made immune to aging and death.

True or False:

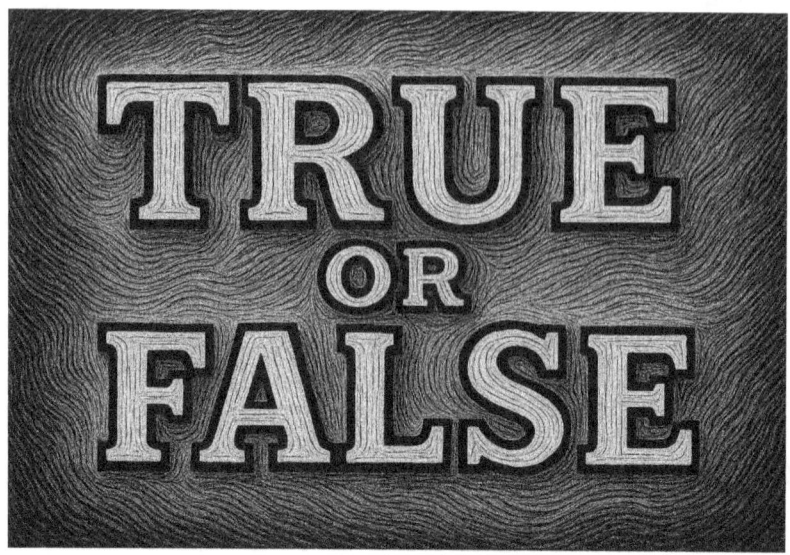

6. True or False: Cain was the older brother of Abel.
7. True or False: Abel offered vegetables as a gift to God.
8. True or False: God was happy with the gift that Cain brought.
9. True or False: Cain killed his brother Abel because he was jealous and angry.
10. True or False: After killing Abel, Cain was not punished by God.

Fill in the Blank:

11. The Bible says that God created humans in His own

    _____.

12. After creating everything, God rested on the _____ day.

13. The serpent told the first woman that if she ate the fruit, she would become like _____.

14. To guard the way to the Tree of Life after they were sent out of the garden, God placed _____ at the east of Eden.

15. As a punishment for what he did to his brother, Cain was made to be a restless _____ on the earth.

Who Said That?

16. "Am I my brother's keeper?" Who said this?

    a) The first man

    b) The first woman

    c) Cain

    d) Abel

17. "Let there be light." Who said these powerful words?

    a) The first man

    b) God

    c) The Serpent

    d) An angel

Bible Book Breakdown:

18. When Adam had lived 130 years, he had a son called _____.

19. After his son was born, Adam lived for _____ more years and had other sons and daughters.

Answers

Multiple Choice Missions

1. c) Light

2. b) Eden

3. b) The Tree of the Knowledge of Good and Evil

4. c) A serpent

5. b) Their eyes were opened, and they realized they were naked.

True or False:

6. True

7. False

8. False

9. True

10. False

Fill in the Blank

11. Image

12. Seventh

13. God

14. Cherubim

15. Wanderer

Who Said That?

16. c) Cain

17. b) God

Bible Book Breakdown:

18. Seth

19. 800

Subsection 2: Noah's Epic Voyage & The Tower That Tried Too Hard!

After the Garden of Eden, several noteworthy events followed, such as a massive flood and a tower with a plan so ambitious it is still known today. Ready to see what you know about Noah's epic boat trip and the Tower of Babel?

Multiple Choice Missions:

1. In Genesis, we see that the world had become pretty messed up, but there was one guy God saw who was living right. Who was he?

   a) Cain's great-great-great-grandson

   b) Methuselah

   c) Noah

   d) Abraham

2. What kind of boat did God tell Noah to build?

   a) A reed boat for river travel

   b) A sturdy merchant ship for trading

   c) A massive wooden ark to preserve life (Noah, his family and the animals on board)

3. How did God get all the animals onto the ark?

   a) Noah had to go out and round them all up.

   b) They showed up on their own in pairs.

   c) The animals were led to the ark by God.

   d) Only certain types of animals were allowed.

4. After the flood, what sign did God give Noah to promise that He'd never flood the whole Earth again?

   a) A dove holding a leaf

   b) A loud voice from the sky

   c) A rainbow

   d) A set of stone tablets

5. What big project did people start after the flood, thinking they could build something that reached heaven?

   a) Building a giant staircase

   b) Stacking large rock piles

   c) A super tall tower

True or False:

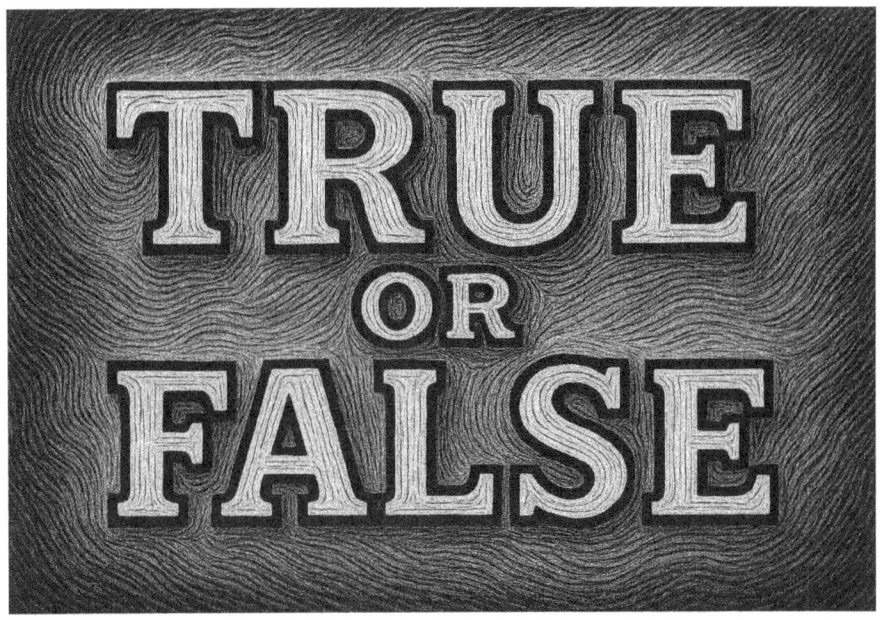

6. True or False: Noah only brought his immediate family onto the ark, together with the animals that were brought inside.

7. True or False: The ark was bigger than any ship we have today.

8. True or False: God was impressed with how united and determined people were to build the Tower of Babel.

9. True or False: The Bible says that because of the Tower of Babel, God made people speak different languages.

10. True or False: The Tower of Babel was finished and reached all the way to Heaven.

Fill in the Blank:

11. God told Noah to build the ark out of _____ wood.

12. Noah sent out _____ to see if the water had gone down.

13. The names of Noah's sons were _____.

14. Before God intervened, everyone building the Tower of Babel spoke the same _____.

15. Because of the tower, God scattered people all over the face of the _____.

Who Said That?

16. "I will never again destroy all living creatures by floodwaters, and never again will there be a flood to destroy the earth." Who made this promise?

    a) Noah

    b) One of Noah's sons

    c) God

    d) Noah's wife

17. "Come, let us build ourselves a city and a tower with its top in the heavens, and let us make a name for ourselves..." What was the main reason behind the Tower of Babel?

    a) To worship God better

    b) To protect themselves from future floods

    c) To glorify themselves and reach Heaven

    d) To see the stars

Bible Book Breakdown:

18. Noah was _____ years old when the floodwater came.

19. According to the Bible, the ark came to rest on the mountains of_____ on the seventeenth day of the seventh month.

Answers:

Multiple Choice Missions

1. c) Noah

2. c) A massive wooden ark to preserve life

3. c) The animals were led to the ark by God.

4. c) A rainbow

5. c) A super tall tower

True or False

6. True

7. False

8. False

9. True

10. False

Fill in the Blank

11. Gopher

12. Dove

13. Shem, Ham, and Japheth

14. Language

15. Earth

Who Said That?

16. c) God

17. c) To make a name for themselves and reach Heaven

Bible Book Breakdown

18. 600

19. Genesis

Subsection 3: From One Family to a Nation

We're still in Genesis, but the story is now focusing on one family that God chose to do some seriously big things through. Get ready to meet Abraham (originally Abram), his wife Sarah (originally Sarai), their son Isaac, Isaac's son Jacob and Jacob's favorite son, Joseph.

Multiple Choice Missions:

1. God made an incredible promise to Abraham (original name Abram), saying his family would grow to be as many as what?

    a) The number of trees in the forest

    b) The grains of sand on a beach

    c) The stars in the sky

2. What was the seemingly impossible thing that God promised Abraham and Sarah when they were already old?

    a) They would become king and queen.

    b) They would travel to every corner of the world.

    c) They would have a child.

3. What was the name of the son born to Abraham and Sarah in their old age? a) Ishmael

    b) Isaac

    c) Jacob

    d) Joseph

4. God tested Abraham's faith with a really tough request. What was he asked to do with Isaac?

    a) Send him away.

    b) Offer him as a sacrifice.

    c) Make him work on the family farm.

5. Jacob had a famous dream about a stairway (or ladder) reaching up to heaven. What was happening on it?

    a) Angels were sliding down it.

    b) People were climbing up.

    c) Angels were going up and down it.

True or False:

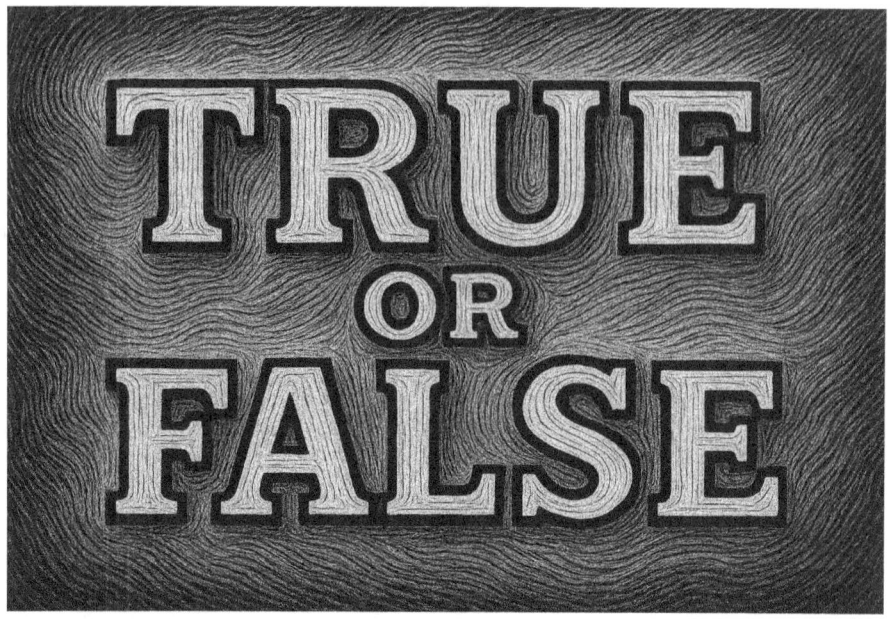

6. True or False: Abraham (Abram) obeyed when God asked him to leave his home.

7. True or False: Sarah (Sarai) always believed God's promise that she would have a child.

8. True or False: Isaac was Abraham's only son.

9. True or False: Jacob tricked his brother Esau out of some important family rights and a blessing.

10. True or False: Joseph's brothers sold him into slavery because they thought his dreams were cool.

Fill in the Blank:

11. God made a special agreement with Abraham, and it was marked by an act of _____.

12. Abraham's original home was in the land of _____.

13. Jacob wrestled with _____ and his name was changed to Israel.

14. God allowed Joseph to interpret_____.

15. In the end, Joseph became a powerful leader in the nation of _____.

Who Said That?

16. "Here I am," Abraham replied. Who was he talking to?

    a) Isaac

    b) Sarah

    c) God

17. "Look, it's still broad daylight; it's not time for the animals to be gathered. Water the sheep and take them back to pasture." Who said this?

    a) Jacob

    b) Leah

    c) Laban

    d) Isaac

Bible Book Breakdown:

18. The Medianites sold Joseph to _____ in Egypt.

19. Joseph told the chief cupbearer his dream of the vine with the three branches meant _____.

Answers

Multiple Choice Missions

1. c) The stars in the sky

2. c) They would have a child.

3. b) Isaac

4. b) Offer him as a sacrifice.

5. c) Angels were going up and down it.

True or False

6. True

7. False

8. False

9. True

10. False

Fill in the Blank

11. Circumcision

12. Ur

13. God

14. Dreams

15. Egypt

Who Said That?

16. c) God

17. a) Jacob

Bible Book Breakdown

18. Potiphar

19. He would be reinstated in his position in three days.

Subsection 4: From Slavery to Exodus - Let My People Go!

From here, the story gets really serious. The family of Abraham, Isaac, and Jacob has grown into a huge group of people in Egypt, but they were now slaves. Although things looked pretty bad, God had a plan, involving a man named Moses. Get ready for burning bushes, plagues, and an escape that changed everything.

Multiple Choice Missions:

1. Why did the Pharaoh of Egypt make the Israelites slaves?

    a) They weren't following his rules.

    b) He was worried they'd grow too numerous and powerful.

    c) He wanted all their belongings.

2. How did God first get Moses' attention?

    a) Through a whisper in the wind.

    b) In a dream.

    c) Through a burning bush that wasn't burning up.

    d) By sending a messenger.

3. What did God tell Moses to demand from Pharaoh?

    a) Land for his people.

    b) To make his people rich.

    c) That the Israelites be allowed to leave with all their belongings.

4. Which one of these was NOT one of the plagues God sent upon Egypt?

    a) Locusts

    b) Darkness

    c) Massive Floods

    d) Frogs

5. What was the really terrible plague that finally made Pharaoh let the Israelites leave?

    a) Famine.

    b) Death of all the farm animals.

    c) The firstborn son in every Egyptian family died.

True or False:

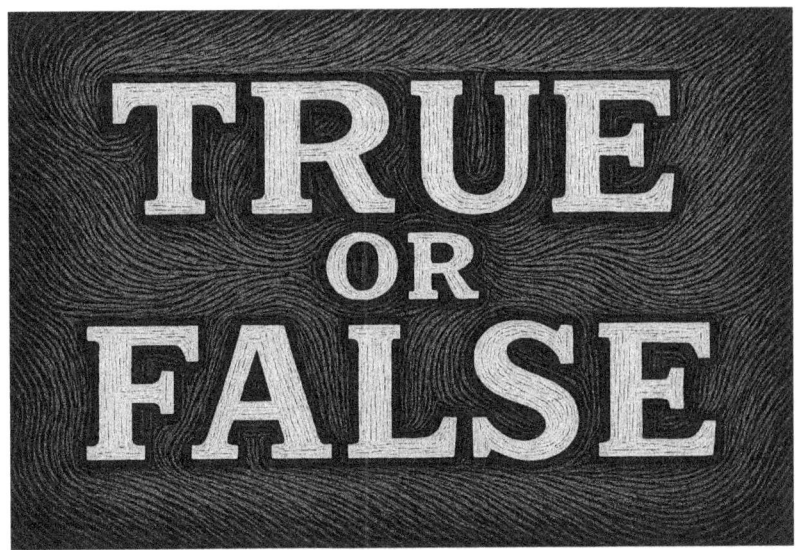

6. True or False: Moses was super excited and felt totally ready to lead the Israelites out of Egypt from the beginning.

7. True or False: Pharaoh let the Israelites go after the very first plague.

8. True or False: The Israelites baked bread without yeast because they had to leave Egypt super fast.

9. True or False: God split apart the water of the Red Sea so the Israelites could walk across on dry land.

10. True or False: Pharaoh himself led his army to chase after the Israelites but decided to turn around before they reached the sea.

Fill in the Blank:

11. Moses' brother, _____, helped him speak to Pharaoh.

12. The festival commemorating when the Israelites left Egypt, after the plague of death on the firstborn, is called _____.

13. God guided the Israelites through the desert with a pillar of _____ during the day and a pillar of _____ at night.

14. The mountain where Moses received the Ten Commandments is called Mount _____.

15. The special tent where the Israelites worshipped God in the desert was called the _____.

Who Said That?

16. "Let my people go, so that they may worship Me in the wilderness."

    Who was asked to give this message to Pharaoh?

    a) Aaron

    b) Moses

    c) Miriam

Bible Book Breakdown:

17. Moses' wife and the mother of his sons Gershom and Eliezer was called _____.

18. Moses was _____ years old when he died.

Answers

Multiple Choice Missions

1. b) He was worried they'd grow too numerous and powerful.

2. c) Through a burning bush that wasn't burning up.

3. c) That the Israelites be allowed to leave with all their belongings.

4. c) Massive Floods

5. c) The firstborn son in every Egyptian family died.

True or False

6. False

7. False

8. True

9. True

10. False

Fill in the Blank

11. Aaron

12. Passover

13. Cloud, Fire

14. Sinai

15. Tabernacle

Who Said That?

16. b) Moses

Bible Book Breakdown

17. Zipporah

18. 120

Subsection 5: Wilderness Wanderings & The Promised Land - The Ultimate Road Trip (With Detours!)

After God's powerful deliverance from Egypt, the Israelites faced a challenging journey to the Promised Land. Their wilderness experience was a spiritual proving ground filled with incredible miracles like food sent from heaven, but also marked by significant complaints and disobedience. Here, we'll explore their time learning God's laws, including the Ten Commandments, as they endured their wanderings before finally stepping into the inheritance God had planned for them

Multiple Choice Missions:

1. What kind of food did God miraculously provide for the Israelites in the desert?

   a) Fruit

   b) Manna

   c) Vegetables

   d) Sunflower seeds

2. According to biblical accounts, what three items were kept inside the Ark of the Covenant?

   a) A golden cup, a scroll of Isaiah, and a bronze serpent.

   b) A jar of manna, Aaron's staff that had budded, and the stone tablets of the covenant.

   c) A copy of the Psalms, a piece of Moses' staff, and a vial of anointing oil.

3. Who took over leading the Israelites after Moses died?

   a) Aaron

   b) Joshua

   c) Caleb

   d) Miriam

4. What river did the Israelites have to cross to get into the Promised Land?

   a) The Nile River

   b) The Amazon River

   c) The Jordan River

   d) The Imperial River

5. What was the first big city the Israelites had to face in the Promised Land?

   a) Jerusalem

   b) Jericho

   c) Bethlehem

   d) Nazareth

True or False:

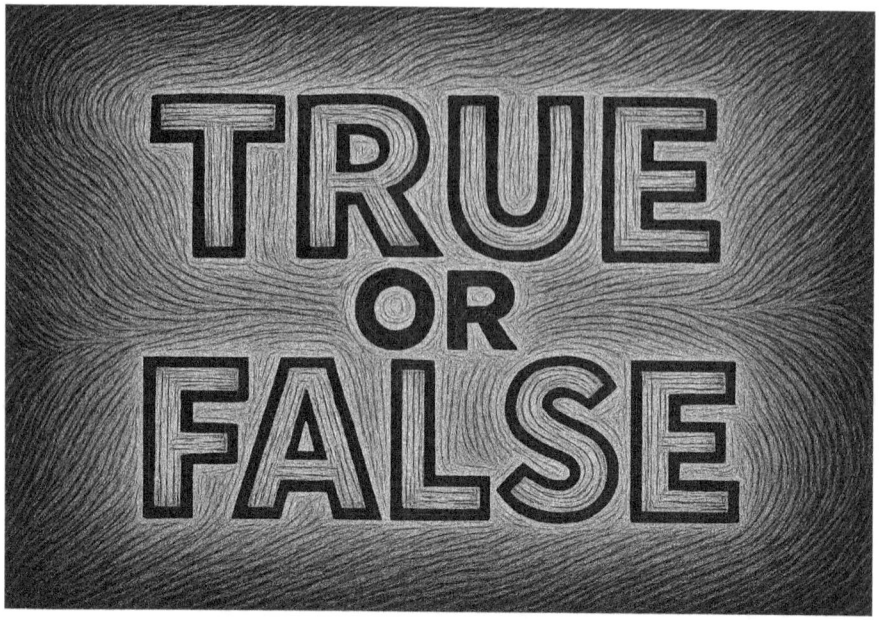

6. True or False: The Israelites were always happy and never complained during their time in the desert.
7. True or False: Moses led the Israelites all the way into the Promised Land.
8. True or False: God gave the Israelites water in the desert by telling Moses to hit a rock with his staff.
9. True or False: The Israelites easily took over the Promised Land without any fighting.
10. True or False: Acacia wood was used to construct the Ark of the Covenant.

Fill in the Blank:

11. The Israelites wandered in the desert for about _____ years.
12. Out of all the spies sent into the Promised Land, only _____ and Caleb said they could take the land.
13. The walls of Jericho fell down after the Israelites marched around the city and the _____ blew their horns.
14. The Promised Land was also called _____.

15. The first book in the Bible after Deuteronomy is _____.

Who Said That?

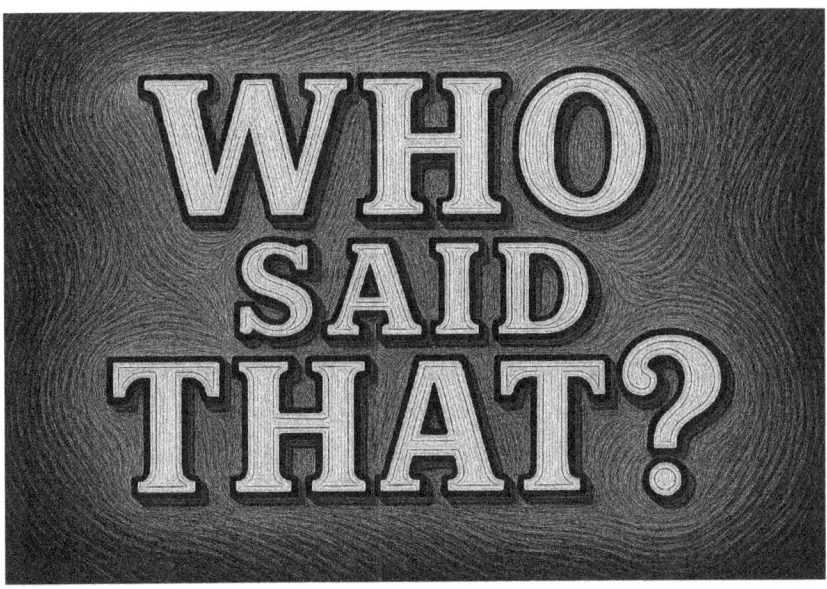

16. "The land we explored is really, really good!" Who said this?

    a) All the spies

    b) Joshua and Caleb

    c) Moses

    d) Aaron

17. "Just as the Lord commanded his servant Moses, so Moses commanded Joshua, and Joshua did it; he left nothing undone of all that the Lord commanded Moses." What does this tell us about Joshua?

    a) He was a great warrior.

    b) He followed God's instructions completely.

    c) He was really popular with the people.

Bible Book Breakdown:

18. Moses took Joshua to stand before _____ and the entire assembly.

19. The seven day long Holy Festival held on the 15th day of the seventh month was called _____.

Answers

Multiple Choice Missions

1. b) Manna

2. b) A jar of manna, Aaron's staff that had budded, and the stone tablets of the covenant.

3. b) Joshua

4. c) The Jordan River

5. b) Jericho

True or False

6. False

7. False

8. True

9. False

10. True

Fill in the Blank

11. Forty

12. Joshua

13. Priests

14. Canaan

15. Joshua

Who Said That?

16. b) Joshua and Caleb

17. b) He followed God's instructions completely.

Bible Book Breakdown

18. Eleazar the priest

19. The Festival of Tabernacles

Subsection 6: Kings, Prophets, and Exile - The Ups and Downs of a Nation

After finally settling into the Promised Land, the Israelites' journey was far from simple. Their story unfolds with incredible highs and devastating lows. Get ready for powerful kings, bold prophets who delivered God's messages, and what awaited the Israelites.

Multiple Choice Missions:

1. Who was the first king of Israel?

    a) David

    b) Solomon

    c) Saul

    d) Samuel

2. Which king of Israel was known for being wise and built the temple in Jerusalem?

    a) Ahab

    b) Hezekiah

    c) Solomon

    d) Josiah

3. What was the job of the prophets in ancient Israel?

    a) To predict the weather.

    b) To entertain the king with stories.

    c) To share God's messages with the people and leaders.

4. Which big empire conquered the northern part of Israel and took its people away?

    a) Egypt

    b) Assyria

    c) Babylon

5. Which prophet had a famous vision of a valley full of dry bones coming back to life, showing that Israel could be restored?

    a) Isaiah

    b) Jeremiah

    c) Ezekiel

    d) Daniel

True or False:

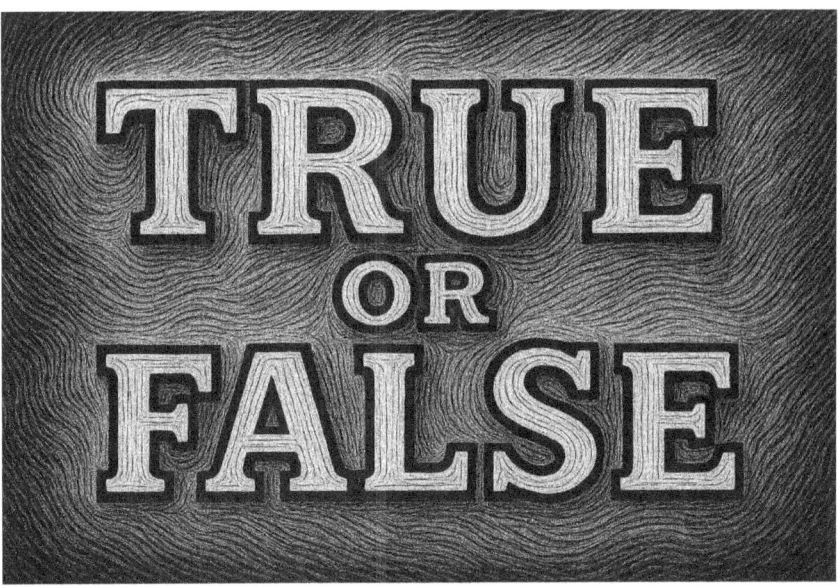

6. True or False: All the kings of Israel and Judah were faithful to God.

7. True or False: The prophet Elijah had a big showdown with false prophets on Mount Carmel.

8. True or False: The southern part of Israel, called Judah, was never taken away into exile.

9. True or False: The prophet Daniel explained dreams for the Babylonian king Nebuchadnezzar.

10. True or False: The Old Testament ends with the Israelites living happily ever after in their own land.

Fill in the Blank:

11. David wrote many of the _____ in the Bible.

12. The northern kingdom of Israel had _____ tribes.

13. The prophet Isaiah talked a lot about the coming _____.

14. The time when the Israelites were forced to live in Babylon lasted for about _____ years.

15. The very last book of the Old Testament is _____.

Who Said That?

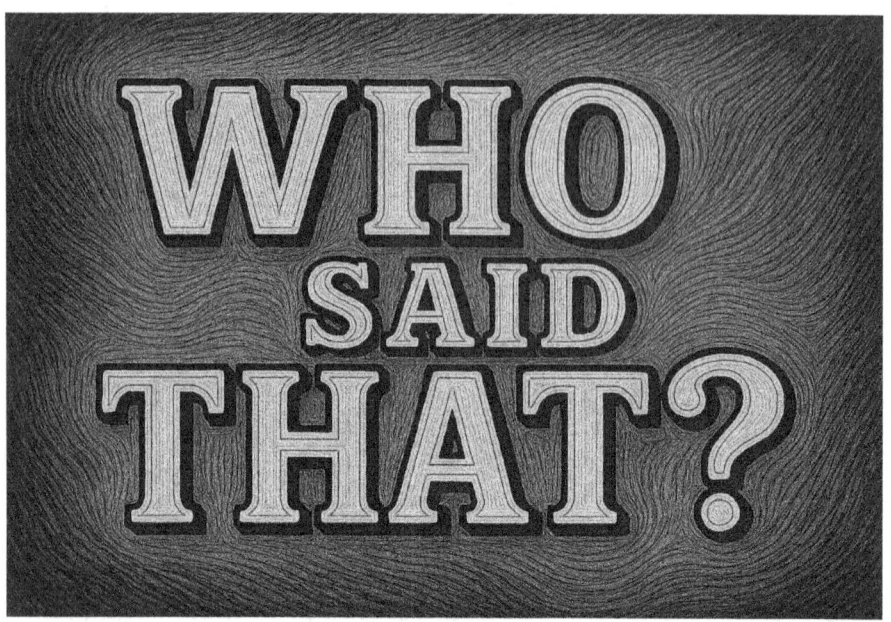

16. "Choose for yourselves this day whom you will serve... But as for me and my household, we will serve the Lord." Who said this?

    a) King David

    b) Prophet Elijah

    c) Joshua

17. "The Lord is my shepherd; I shall not want." These famous words are from which book and who wrote them?

    a) Proverbs, King Solomon

    b) Psalms, King David

    c) Isaiah, the Prophet

Bible Book Breakdown:

18. The books that tell the history of Israel's kings and prophets include 1 and 2 Samuel, 1 and 2 Kings, and 1 and 2 _____.

19. The major books written by prophets in the Old Testament include Isaiah, Jeremiah, Ezekiel, and _____.

Answers

Multiple Choice Missions

1. c) Saul

2. c) Solomon

3. c) To share God's messages with the people and leaders.

4. b) Assyria

5. c) Ezekiel

True or False

6. False

7. True

8. False

9. True

10. False

Fill in the Blank

11. Psalms

12. Ten

13. Messiah

14. Seventy

15. Malachi

Who Said That?

16. c) Joshua

17. b) Psalms, King David

Bible Book Breakdown

18. Chronicles

19. Daniel

Subsection 7: Jesus and the Gospels - The Main Event Begins!

Everything in the Old Testament was leading up to this: Meeting Jesus, the Son of God, whose life, teachings, death, and coming back to life are the most important parts of the Bible. This section focuses on the first four books of the New Testament.

Multiple Choice Missions:

1. In what town was Jesus born?

    a) Jerusalem

    b) Bethlehem

    c) Nazareth

    d) Capernaum

2. Who baptized Jesus in the Jordan River?

    a) Peter

    b) John the Baptist

    c) Mary Magdalene

3. How many main followers (disciples) did Jesus choose?

    a) 7

    b) 12

    c) 20

4. What was the main message Jesus taught?

    a) How to get rich

    b) Following all the rules perfectly

    c) Loving God and loving others

5. What are the stories Jesus often used to teach spiritual lessons called?

    a) Legends

    b) Myths

    c) Parables

True or False:

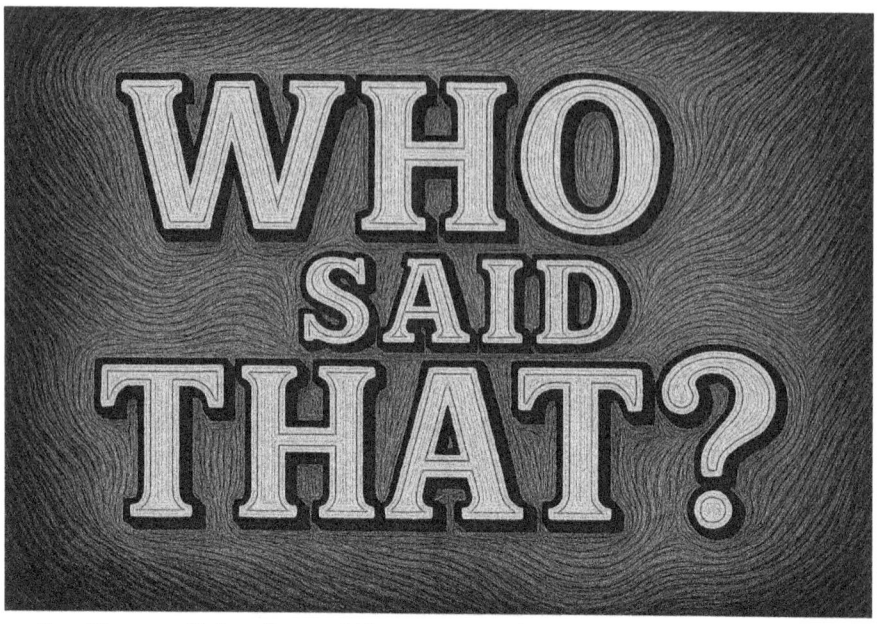

6. True or False: Jesus did many amazing miracles that showed God's power.

7. True or False: Everyone Jesus met liked and respected him.

8. True or False: Jesus taught his followers the "Our Father" prayer.

9. True or False: Jesus died on a cross, was entombed, and then came back to life three days later.

10. True or False: All four books about Jesus tell the exact same story with no differences.

Fill in the Blank:

11. The first four books of the New Testament are Matthew, Mark, _____, and John.

12. Jesus often called himself the _____ of Man.

13. The last meal Jesus shared with his disciples before he died is called the Last _____.

14. The Roman governor who sentenced Jesus to death was Pontius _____.

15. Christians celebrate Jesus coming back to life on _____.

Who Said That?

16. "You are the Christ, the Son of the living God." Who said this about Jesus?

    a) Judas Iscariot

    b) Peter

    c) Mary, Jesus' mother

17. "For God so loved the world that he gave his one and only Son, that whoever believes in him shall not perish but have eternal life." This famous verse is in which book?

    a) Matthew

    b) Mark

    c) John

Bible Book Breakdown:

18. The book about Jesus that is often thought to be written for Jewish people, showing him as the Messiah, is _____.

19. The book about Jesus that is known for being fast-paced and focusing on his actions is _____.

Answers

Multiple Choice Missions

1. b) Bethlehem

2. b) John the Baptist

3. b) 12

4. c) Loving God and loving others

5. c) Parables

True or False Trials

6. True

7. False

8. True

9. True

10. False

Fill in the Blank

11. Luke

12. Son

13. Supper

14. Pilate

15. Easter

Who Said That?

16. b) Peter

17. c) John

Bible Book Breakdown

18. Matthew

19. Mark

Subsection 8: The Early Church and Revelation - The Story Continues

Jesus went back to Heaven, but his followers, filled with God's Spirit, kept doing His work. Get ready for the start of the church, journeys to spread the word, letters of encouragement and correction, and a look into the future in the book of Revelation.

Multiple Choice Missions:

1. What big event happened on the Day of Pentecost?

   a) Jesus went back to Heaven.

   b) The Holy Spirit came upon Jesus' followers.

   c) The first church building was opened.

2. Who was a key leader in the early church who traveled around telling people about Jesus?

   a) Peter

   b) Paul

   c) James

3. What were the letters written by Paul and other leaders mostly about?

   a) Fables.

   b) Telling travel stories.

   c) Encouraging and teaching the first Christians.

4. What is the very last book of the Bible?

   a) Acts

   b) Romans

   c) Revelation

5. What is the book of Revelation mainly about?

   a) Biographies of all the apostles.

   b) How to build churches.

   c) Symbolic visions about the end of the world and God winning in the end.

True or False:

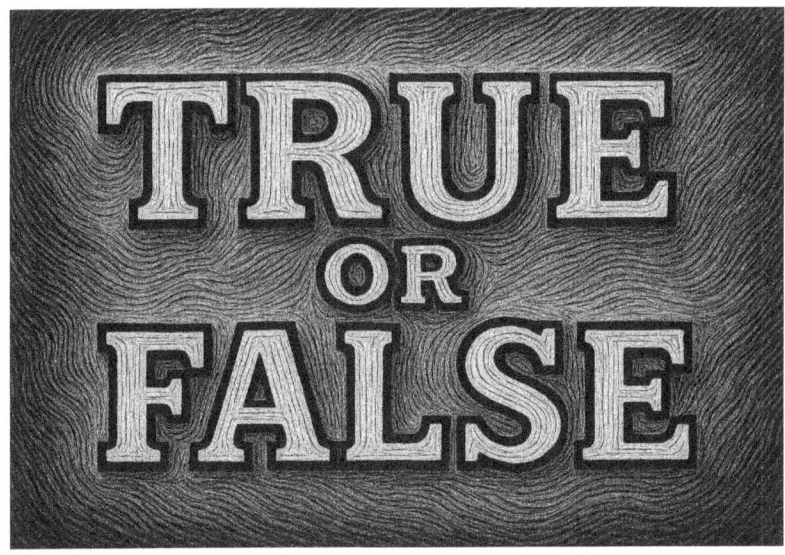

6. True or False: The first Christians had no problems or mean people bothering them.
7. True or False: Paul used to be against Christians before he became one himself.
8. True or False: The book of Acts mostly talks about how the church grew in Jerusalem.
9. True or False: The book of Revelation should be taken as a literal, step-by-step prediction of the future by everyone.
10. True or False: The Bible ends with a hopeful message about God's lasting rule.

Fill in the Blank:

11. The disciple who gave the first big speech on the Day of Pentecost was _____.
12. Paul's big change of heart happened on the road to _____.
13. The city where the first big meeting of church leaders happened to talk about non-Jewish believers was _____.
14. The person who wrote the book of Revelation is usually thought to be the apostle _____.
15. The New Testament ends with a promise of Jesus coming back and God creating a new _____ and a new earth.

Who Said That?

16. "Repent and be baptized, every one of you, in the name of Jesus Christ for the forgiveness of your sins. And you will receive the gift of the Holy Spirit." Who said this?

    a) Paul

    b) Peter

17. "I have fought the good fight, I have finished the race, I have kept the faith." These are thought to be the last words of which apostle before he died?

    a) Peter

    b) Paul

Bible Book Breakdown:

18. The book that tells the story of what happened after Jesus went back to heaven and the church started is _____.

19. The letters written by Paul are called _____.

Answers

Multiple Choice Missions

1. b) The Holy Spirit came upon Jesus' followers.

2. b) Paul

3. c) Encouraging and teaching the first Christians.

4. c) Revelation

5. c) Symbolic visions about the end of the world and God winning in the end.

True or False

6. False

7. True

8. False

9. False

10. True

Fill in the Blank

11. Peter

12. Damascus

13. Antioch

14. John

15. Heaven

Who Said That?

16. b) Peter

17. b) Paul

Bible Book Breakdown

18. Acts

19. Epistles

Section 2: Awesome People of the Bible

Subsection 1: The Faith Hall of Famers (Old Testament Heroes)

The Old Testament has several incredible stories of people who trusted God in amazing ways, even when things got tough. These "Faith Hall of Famers" faced huge challenges, made some mistakes, but their stories teach us a lot about what it means to follow God.

Multiple Choice Missions:

1. What was away Abraham showed his trust in God?

   a) By always having the best sacrifices.

   b) By immediately obeying God's call to leave his homeland.

   c) By arguing with God whenever he disagreed.

   d) By becoming the richest person in his region.

2. Moses led the Israelites out of Egypt. What was his initial reaction when God asked him to do this?

   a) He was excited and ready to go.

   b) He felt unqualified and made excuses.

   c) He asked for a sign to prove God was real.

   d) He immediately went to Pharaoh.

3. King David wasn't just a king; he was also known for something else he did. What was it?

   a) He was a great architect.

   b) He was a skilled musician and songwriter (many of the Psalms!).

   c) He was a famous inventor.

   d) He was a powerful military general from a young age.

4. Ruth was a Moabite woman who showed incredible loyalty. To whom was she fiercely loyal?

   a) Her former gods.

   b) The king of Moab.

   c) Her mother-in-law, Naomi.

   d) The other women in her village.

5. Esther became queen of Persia. What brave thing did she do to help her people?

   a) She started a rebellion against the king.

   b) She hid her identity and risked her life to speak to the king.

   c) She used her wealth to bribe the king's officials.

   d) She escaped and warned her people from afar.

True or False:

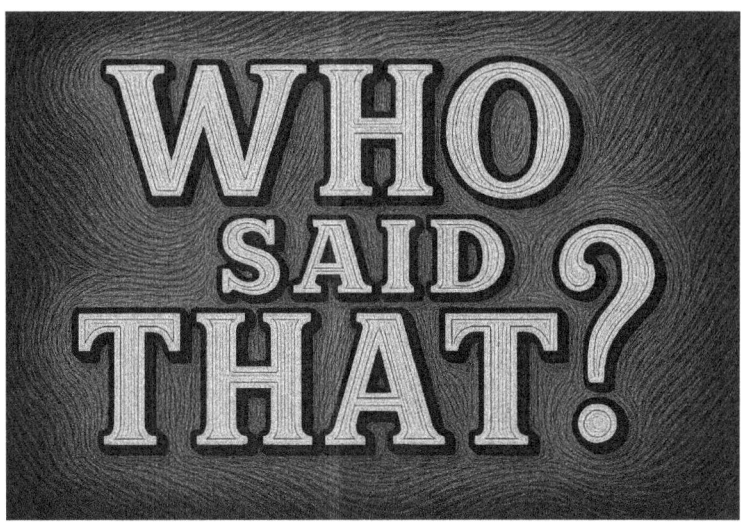

6. True or False: Abraham never doubted God's promises.
7. True or False: Moses was a confident and skilled public speaker from the beginning of his mission.
8. True or False: David never made any mistakes or sinned during his reign as king.
9. True or False: Ruth chose to return to her homeland after her husband died.
10. True or False: Esther's uncle Mordecai encouraged her to hide her Jewish identity.

Fill in the Blank:

11. God promised Abraham that his descendants would be as numerous as the _____ in the sky.
12. Moses performed many miracles using the _____ that God gave him.
13. David famously defeated the giant _____ with a slingshot and stones.
14. Ruth's famous declaration of loyalty to Naomi included the words, "Your people will be my people, and your _____ my _____."
15. Esther's courage led to the celebration of the Jewish festival of _____.

Who Am I?

16. I was willing to sacrifice my beloved son because God asked me to. My faith was tested in a big way. Who am I?

    a) Moses

    b) Abraham

    c) David

    d) Noah

17. I led my people out of slavery, but I wasn't allowed to enter the Promised Land myself. Who am I?

    a) Joshua

    b) Moses

    c) Abraham

    d) Joseph

Bible Book Breakdown:

18. The story of Abraham's early life and God's covenant with him is mainly found in the book of _____.

19. The story of Ruth and her loyalty is told in the book of _____.

Answers

Multiple Choice Missions

1. b) By immediately obeying God's call to leave his homeland.

2. b) He felt unqualified and made excuses.

3. b) He was a skilled musician and songwriter (many of the Psalms!).

4. c) Her mother-in-law, Naomi.

5. b) She hid her identity and risked her life to speak to the king.

True or False

6. False

7. False

8. False

9. False

10. False

Fill in the Blank

11. stars

12. staff

13. Goliath

14. God, God

15. Purim

Who Said That?

16. b) Abraham

17. b) Moses

Bible Book Breakdown

18. Genesis

19. Ruth

Subsection 2: Jesus' Inner Circle - The Twelve Disciples

Jesus chose 12 disciples that walked with him, learned from him, and were sent out to share his message. These disciples came from different walks of life, and their stories are part of the Biblical history that we know today.

Multiple Choice Missions:

1. Which of Jesus' disciples was a fisherman and often considered the leader of the group?

    a) John

    b) Peter

    c) James

    d) Andrew

2. Which disciple was a tax collector before following Jesus?

    a) Simon the Zealot

    b) Matthew

    c) Philip

    d) Thomas

3. Which two disciples were brothers and known for their fiery personalities (Jesus even nicknamed them "Sons of Thunder")?

    a) Peter and Andrew

    b) James and John

    c) Philip and Bartholomew

    d) Thaddeus and Simon

4. Which disciple is famous for doubting Jesus' resurrection until he saw him with his own eyes?

    a) James

    b) Thomas

    c) Matthew

    d) Judas

5. Which disciple betrayed Jesus for thirty pieces of silver?

    a) Peter

    b) John

    c) Judas Iscariot

    d) Philip

True or False:

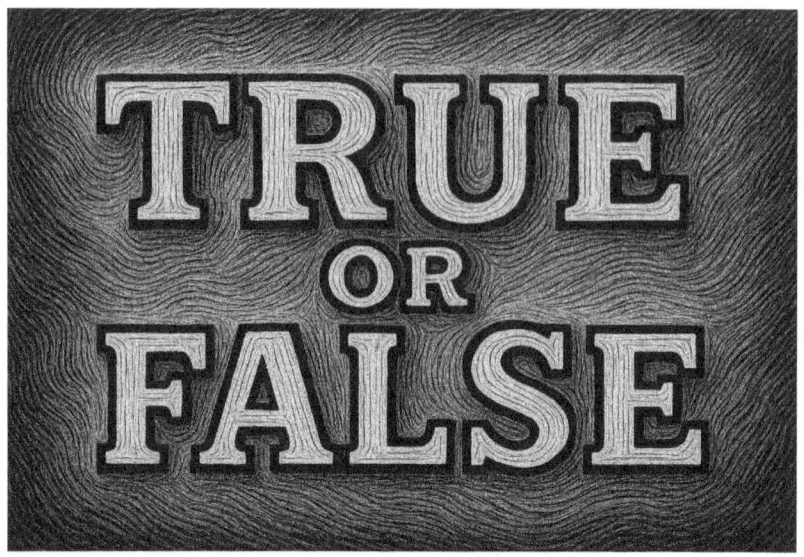

6. True or False: All twelve disciples were quick to understand Jesus' teachings.

7. True or False: Peter walked on water just like Jesus did.

8. True or False: John was known as "the disciple whom Jesus loved."

9. True or False: Matthew kept his tax collector job while following Jesus.

10. True or False: After Jesus' ascension, all twelve disciples remained in Jerusalem.

Fill in the Blank:

11. Peter's original name was _____.

12. Andrew was Peter's _____.

13. James and John were the sons of _____.

14. Philip brought his friend _____ to meet Jesus.

15. Thomas said he wouldn't believe Jesus had risen unless he saw the nail marks in his _____ and put his finger where the nails had been.

Who Am I?

16. I denied knowing Jesus three times, even though I had promised to follow him anywhere. Who am I?

    a) John

    b) Peter

    c) James

    d) Thomas

17. I was in charge of the money bag for the disciples and sometimes helped myself to it. Who am I?

    a) Matthew

    b) Philip

    c) Judas Iscariot

    d) Simon the Zealot

Bible Book Breakdown:

18. The stories of Jesus calling his disciples and their early ministry are found in the Gospels of Matthew, Mark, _____, and John.

19. The book of _____ tells about what the disciples did after Jesus ascended to heaven.

Answers

Multiple Choice Missions

1. b) Peter

2. b) Matthew

3. b) James and John

4. b) Thomas

5. c) Judas Iscariot

True or False

6. False

7. True

8. True

9. False

10. False

Fill in the Blank

11. Simon

12. brother

13. Zebedee

14. Nathanael

15. hands

Who Said That?

16. b) Peter

17. c) Judas Iscariot

Bible Book Breakdown

18. Luke

19. Acts

Subsection 3: Game Changers - Other Influential People

The Bible isn't just about the big heroes and the 12 disciples. There are others who played important roles in God's story. This part highlights some of these "Game Changers": people who, in their own way, significantly impacted the narrative of faith.

Multiple Choice Missions:

1. Mary Magdalene was one of Jesus' devoted followers. What special privilege did she have after his resurrection?

    a) She performed the first miracle after Jesus rose.

    b) She was the first person Jesus appeared to after rising from the dead.

    c) She became the leader of the early church.

    d) She wrote one of the Gospels.

2. Paul (originally Saul) was a major figure in the early church. What was he doing before he became a follower of Jesus?

    a) He was a Roman soldier.

    b) He was a fisherman alongside Peter.

    c) He was actively persecuting Christians.

    d) He was a tax collector.

3. Deborah was a unique leader in the Old Testament. What role did she primarily serve?

    a) She was a queen.

    b) She was a prophet and a judge.

    c) She was a military commander.

    d) She was a musician in the temple.

4. Elijah was a powerful prophet in the Old Testament. What dramatic event marked the end of his earthly ministry?

    a) He was stoned by his enemies.

    b) He died of old age surrounded by his followers.

    c) He was taken up to heaven in a whirlwind.

    d) He was thrown into a lions' den.

5. Timothy was a young man who became a close companion and helper of which apostle?

    a) Peter

    b) John

    c) Paul

    d) James

True or False:

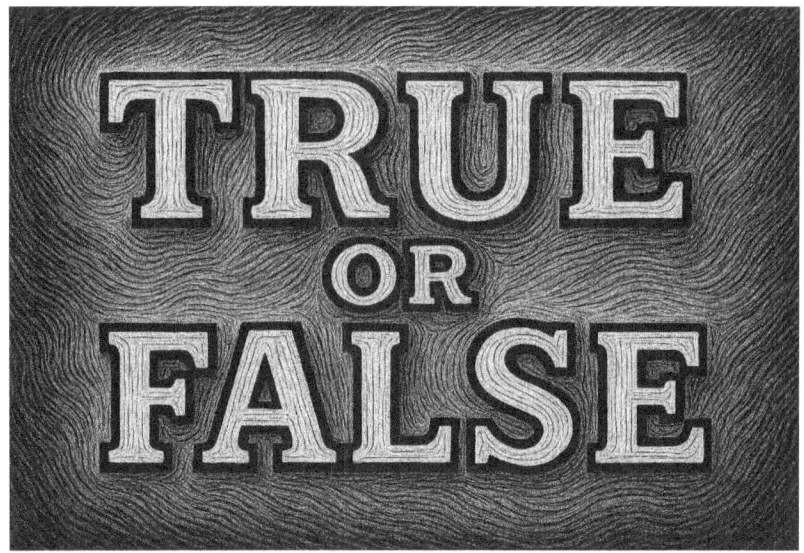

6. True or False: Mary, the mother of Jesus, played no significant role in his ministry after his birth.

7. True or False: Paul was never imprisoned for his faith.

8. True or False: Deborah personally led the Israelite army into battle.

9. True or False: Elijah performed many miracles, including raising someone from the dead.

10. True or False: Timothy was older than Paul.

Fill in the Blank:

11. Mary Magdalene was among the women who first visited Jesus' _____ after his crucifixion.

12. Paul wrote many _____ that are now part of the New Testament.

13. Deborah prophesied that the commander Barak would only achieve victory if she went with him into _____.

14. Elijah challenged the prophets of _____ to a contest on Mount Carmel.

15. Paul wrote two letters specifically addressed to _____, giving him guidance for church leadership.

Who Am I?

16. I was a woman who supported Jesus' ministry financially and was present at his crucifixion and resurrection. Who am I?

    a) Mary, the mother of Jesus

    b) Martha

    c) Mary Magdalene

    d) Salome

17. I was a powerful speaker and a key figure in the early church in Alexandria, known for my eloquent teaching. Who am I?

    a) Barnabas

    b) Apollos

    c) Silas

    d) Luke

Bible Book Breakdown:

18. The stories of Mary Magdalene's encounters with the risen Jesus are found in all four _____.

19. Many of Paul's letters, including those to Timothy, are found in the _____ Testament.

Answers

Multiple Choice Missions

1. b) She was the first person Jesus appeared to after rising from the dead.

2. c) He was actively persecuting Christians.

3. b) She was a prophet and a judge.

4. c) He was taken up to heaven in a whirlwind.

5. c) Paul

True or False

6. False

7. False

8. False

9. True

10. False

Fill in the Blank

11. tomb

12. letters

13. Mount Tabor

14. Baal

15. Timothy

Who Said That?

16. c) Mary Magdalene

17. b) Apollos

Bible Book Breakdown

18. Gospels

19. New

Subsection 4: Tricky Tales - Complex or Controversial Figures

The Bible doesn't shy away from flawed individuals and complex stories. This part looks at people whose lives raise tough questions or whose actions were a mix of good and bad. Exploring these figures helps us understand that faith isn't always simple and that God can work through imperfect people.

Multiple Choice Missions:

1. Samson was known for his incredible strength. What was the source of his power?

   a) Special armor he wore.

   b) A magic potion he drank.

   c) His uncut hair, as part of a vow to God.

   d) His intense physical training.

2. Jonah was a prophet who disobeyed God's command. What was he told to do?

   a) To go and preach to the city of Jerusalem.

   b) To go and preach to the city of Nineveh.

   c) To go and preach to the Israelites in exile.

   d) To go and preach to the Pharaoh of Egypt.

3. King Solomon was known for his wisdom, but he also made some questionable choices. What was one of his major downfalls?

   a) He lost all his wealth.

   b) He angered God by marrying many foreign women and allowing the worship of their gods.

   c) He became a cruel and unjust ruler.

   d) He stopped believing in God.

4. Saul was the first king of Israel. Why did God eventually reject him as king?

   a) He was too kind to his enemies.

   b) He disobeyed God's direct commands.

   c) He wasn't a good military leader.

   d) He tried to make himself a prophet.

5. Judas Iscariot's motives for betraying Jesus are debated. What is one possible reason mentioned in the Bible?

   a) He hated Jesus' teachings.

   b) He was promised a large sum of money.

   c) He wanted to force Jesus to start a rebellion.

   d) All of the above.

True or False:

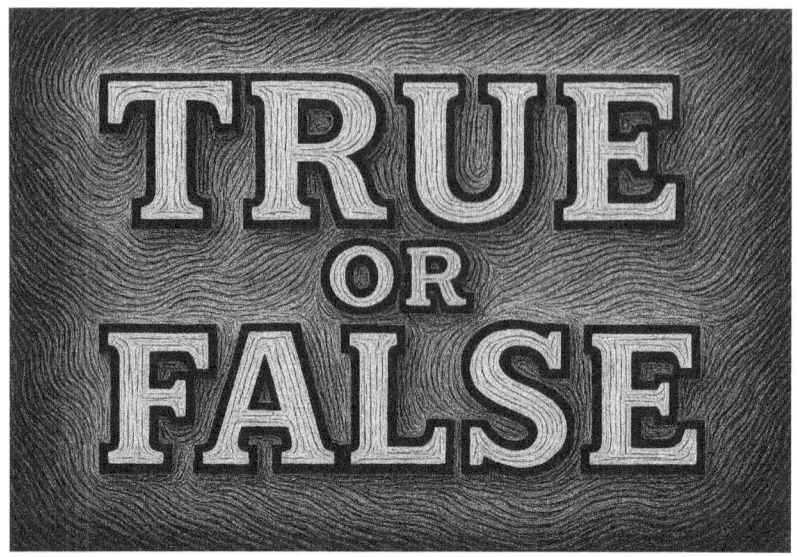

6. True or False: Samson always used his strength for good.

7. True or False: Jonah was happy to go to Nineveh after he was rescued from the big fish.

8. True or False: Solomon remained faithful to God throughout his entire life.

9. True or False: Saul humbly accepted God's decision to replace him as king.

10. True or False: The Bible clearly states that Judas betrayed Jesus solely for the money.

Fill in the Blank:

11. Samson was ultimately betrayed by _____ who cut his hair.

12. Jonah was swallowed by a _____ when he tried to run away from God.

13. Solomon's wisdom is highlighted in the story of how he settled a dispute between two _____.

14. Saul tried to kill _____ out of jealousy.

15. After betraying Jesus, Judas felt great remorse and _____ himself.

Who Am I?

16. I was incredibly strong, but my weakness for a woman led to my downfall. Who am I?

    a) Solomon

    b) Samson

    c) Saul

    d) Jonah

17. I was a king known for my wisdom, but I also allowed idol worship in Israel. Who am I?

    a) David

    b) Solomon

    c) Hezekiah

    d) Josiah

Bible Book Breakdown:

18. The story of Samson and his strength is found in the book of _____.

19. The story of Jonah and the big fish is told in the book of _____.

Answers

Multiple Choice Missions

1. c) His uncut hair, as part of a vow to God.

2. b) To go and preach to the city of Nineveh.

3. b) He angered God by marrying many foreign women and allowing the worship of their gods.

4. b) He disobeyed God's direct commands.

5. b) He was promised a large sum of money.

True or False

6. False

7. False

8. False

9. False

10. False

Fill in the Blank:

11. Delilah

12. large fish

13. prostitutes

14. David

15. hanged

Who Said That?

16. b) Samson

17. b) Solomon

Bible Book Breakdown

18. Judges

19. Jonah

Section 3: Theme Park - Exploring Key Biblical Themes

Subsection 1: Love & Relationships (God's love, friendship, family)

This section explores crucial connections: from the unconditional love God has for us, to the rock-solid bonds of true friendship, and even the seriously complicated dynamics within families. Get ready to gain a fresh perspective on how to navigate your own connections.

Multiple Choice Missions:

1. The Bible often describes God's love for humanity using what powerful comparison?

    a) Like a strict teacher for their students.

    b) Like a distant king for their subjects.

    c) Like a loving parent for their child.

    d) Like a ship captain to a crew.

2. Who in the Old Testament is known for their incredibly close and loyal friendship?

    a) Abraham and Lot

    b) Moses and Aaron

    c) David and Jonathan

    d) Jacob and Esau

3. The story of the prodigal son is a powerful illustration of what aspect of God's love?

    a) His preference for those who always obey.

    b) His anger towards those who mess up.

    c) His forgiving and welcoming nature.

    d) His desire for perfect people.

4. What is often referred to as the "greatest commandment" by Jesus?

    a) To always attend religious services.

    b) To follow all the rules perfectly.

    c) To love God with all your heart and to love your neighbor as yourself.

    d) To give all your money to the poor.

5. The Bible emphasizes the importance of unity and love within the Christian community. What analogy does it sometimes use to describe this?

    a) Like individual trees in a forest.

    b) Like different instruments in an orchestra.

    c) Like separate islands in an ocean.

    d) Like scattered stones on a beach.

True or False:

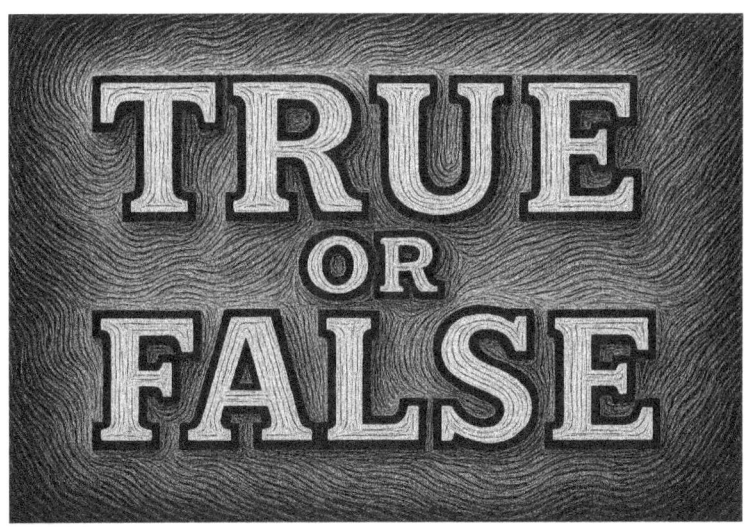

6. True or False: God's love is conditional; we have to earn it by being good.

7. True or False: The friendship between David and Jonathan faced no challenges.

8. True or False: In the story of the prodigal son, the older brother was very happy about his younger brother's return.

9. True or False: Jesus taught that loving your enemies is impossible.

10. True or False: The Bible encourages believers to isolate themselves from non-believers to maintain their purity.

Fill in the Blank:

11. "For God so _____ the world that he gave his one and only Son..." (John 3:16)

12. Jonathan showed his love for David by giving him his robe, his tunic, his sword, his bow, and his _____.

13. When the prodigal son returned home, his father _____ him and kissed him.

14. Jesus said, "A new command I give you: Love one another. As I have loved you, so you must _____ one another." (John 13:34)

15. "Be completely humble and gentle; be patient, bearing with one another in _____." (Ephesians 4:2)

Who Said That?

16. "Where you go I will go, and where you stay I will stay. Your people will be my people and your God my God." Who said this as an expression of deep loyalty and love?

　　a) Ruth to Naomi

　　b) David to Jonathan

　　c) The prodigal son to his father

　　d) Esther to Mordecai

17. "Greater love has no one than this: to lay down one's life for one's friends." Who said this?

　　a) Paul

　　b) Peter

　　c) Jesus

　　d) John

Bible Book Breakdown:

18. The story of the deep friendship between David and Jonathan is primarily found in the book of _____.

19. Jesus' teachings about love are central to all four _____.

Answers

Multiple Choice Missions

1. c) Like a loving parent for their child.

2. c) David and Jonathan

3. c) His forgiving and welcoming nature.

4. c) To love God with all your heart and to love your neighbor as yourself.

5. b) Like different instruments in an orchestra.

True or False

6. False

7. False

8. False

9. False

10. False

Fill in the Blank

11. loved

12. robe

13. hugged/embraced

14. love

15. patience

Who Said That?

16. a) Ruth to Naomi

17. c) Jesus

Bible Book Breakdown:

18. 1 Samuel/2 Samuel

19. Gospels

Subsection 2: Forgiveness & Redemption (Second chances, grace)

The Bible has powerful stories of second chances and how God offers forgiveness and redemption, even when people mess up big time. This section explores this important theme.

Multiple Choice Missions:

1. After denying Jesus three times, which disciple was eventually restored and became a key leader in the early church?

    a) Judas Iscariot

    b) Thomas

    c) Peter

    d) John

2. The story of the woman caught in adultery, whom the religious leaders wanted to stone, highlights what aspect of Jesus' character?

    a) His strict adherence to the law.

    b) His fear of public opinion.

    c) His compassion and offer of forgiveness.

3. The parable of the lost sheep illustrates God's attitude towards those who wander away. What does the shepherd do when he realizes a sheep is missing?

    a) He blames the lost sheep.

    b) He ignores the lost sheep and focuses on the others.

    c) He leaves the ninety-nine to search for the one lost sheep.

    d) He punishes the other sheep for not keeping watch.

4. Paul, who wrote many books in the New Testament, had a past of doing what to Christians before his conversion?

    a) Praising them publicly.

    b) Ignoring them completely.

    c) Actively persecuting and imprisoning them.

    d) Secretly helping them.

5. The concept of "grace" in the Bible refers to what?

    a) Earning God's favor through good deeds.

    b) God's unearned and undeserved favor.

    c) God's obligation to forgive everyone.

    d) God only helping perfect people.

True or False:

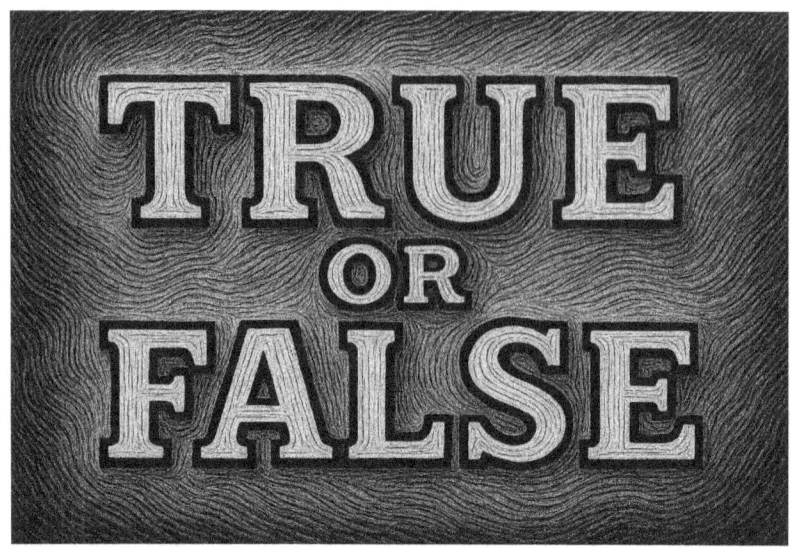

6. True or False: Peter never fully recovered from the shame of denying Jesus.

7. True or False: Jesus told the woman caught in adultery that her sin was acceptable.

8. True or False: The parable of the lost sheep emphasizes the value God places on each individual.

9. True or False: Paul's past actions were held against him by the other apostles and early Christians.

10. True or False: Grace means God overlooks our sins without any consequences.

Fill in the Blank:

11. When Peter denied Jesus, a _____ crowed.

12. Jesus told the woman caught in adultery, "Go now and leave your life of _____." (John 8:11)

13. In the parable of the lost sheep, there is more rejoicing in heaven over one sinner who _____ than over ninety-nine righteous persons who do not need to repent. (Luke 15:7)

14. Paul's _____ happened on the road to Damascus

15. "For it is by _____ you have been saved, through faith—and this is not from yourselves, it is the gift of God." (Ephesians 2:8)

Who Said That?

16. "Father, forgive them, for they do not know what they are doing." Who said this while being crucified?

   a) Peter

   b) Paul

   c) Jesus

   d) One of the criminals crucified with Jesus

17. "Even though I was once a blasphemer and a persecutor and a violent man, I was shown mercy because I acted in ignorance and unbelief." Who wrote these words reflecting on their past?

   a) Peter

   b) Paul

   c) John

   d) James

Bible Book Breakdown:

18. The story of Peter's denial and restoration is found in all four _____.

19. Paul's conversion and his teachings on grace are prominent in his letters, especially the book of _____.

Answers

Multiple Choice Missions

1. c) Peter

2. c) His compassion and offer of forgiveness.

3. c) He leaves the ninety-nine to search for the one lost sheep.

4. c) Actively persecuting and imprisoning them.

5. b) God's unearned and undeserved favor.

True or False

6. False

7. False

8. True

9. False

10. False

Fill in the Blank

11. rooster/cock

12. sin

13. repents

14. conversion

15. grace

Who Said That?

16. c) Jesus

17. b) Paul

Bible Book Breakdown

18. Gospels

19. Romans

Subsection 3: Faith & Trust (Believing in God, even when it's hard)

Throughout the Bible, we see examples of people who had strong faith and trusted God, even in difficult or seemingly impossible situations. This section explores what it means to have faith and trust in God.

Multiple Choice Missions:

1. Abraham is a prime example of faith. What specific act is often highlighted as his ultimate test of trust in God?

    a) Building an altar to God.

    b) Leaving his homeland.

    c) Being willing to sacrifice his son Isaac.

    d) Arguing with God about Sodom and Gomorrah.

2. When the Israelites were trapped between the Egyptian army and the Red Sea, what did Moses tell them to do?

    a) Surrender to the Egyptians.

    b) Try to swim across the sea.

    c) Stand firm and see the deliverance the Lord would bring.

    d) Build boats to escape.

3. Daniel showed great faith by continuing to pray to God even when it was against the king's decree. What was the consequence of his faith?

    a) He was promoted to a higher position.

    b) He was thrown into a fiery furnace.

    c) He was thrown into a lions' den.

    d) He was exiled from the kingdom.

4. Jesus often told his followers that their faith had healed them. What does this suggest about the role of faith in experiencing God's power?

    a) Faith forces God to act.

    b) God only helps those with perfect faith.

    c) Faith is often a key element in receiving what God offers.

    d) God acts regardless of whether people believe.

5. The book of Hebrews talks about faith as being sure of what we hope for and certain of what we do not see. What does this imply about faith?

    a) It's based on visible evidence.

    b) It requires understanding everything perfectly.

    c) It involves believing in things that aren't yet tangible.

    d) It's the same as wishful thinking.

True or False:

6. True or False: Abraham fully understood God's plan for his descendants when he was first called.

7. True or False: The Israelites were always confident and trusting in God during their wilderness journey.

8. True or False: Daniel's faith protected him from any harm in the lions' den.

9. True or False: Jesus only healed people who had a lot of religious knowledge.

10. True or False: The Bible teaches that doubt and faith cannot coexist.

Fill in the Blank:

11. By _____ Abraham obeyed when God called him to go to a place he would later receive as his inheritance. (Hebrews 11:8)

12. When Moses stretched out his hand over the Red Sea, the Lord drove the sea back with a strong _____ wind and turned it into dry land. (Exodus 14:21)

13. Daniel continued to get down on his knees three times a day to pray and give thanks to his God, just as he had done _____. (Daniel 6:10)

14. Jesus often said, "Your _____ has healed you; go in peace." (e.g., Luke 8:48)

15. "Without _____ it is impossible to please God, because anyone who comes to him must believe that he exists and that he rewards those who earnestly seek him." (Hebrews 11:6)

Who Said That?

16. "But without faith it is impossible to please God..." Who wrote these words emphasizing the importance of faith?

    a) Peter

    b) Paul (the author of Hebrews is traditionally attributed to Paul or someone in his circle)

    c) James

    d) John

17. "Lord, I believe; help my unbelief!" Who said this, expressing a struggle between faith and doubt?

    a) Abraham

    b) Moses

    c) The father of a possessed boy

    d) Thomas

Bible Book Breakdown:

18. The story of Abraham's test of faith is primarily found in the book of _____.

19. The book of _____ is often called the "hall of faith" for its examples of those who trusted God.

Answers

Multiple Choice Missions

1. c) Being willing to sacrifice his son Isaac.

2. c) Stand firm and see the deliverance the Lord would bring.

3. c) He was thrown into a lions' den.

4. c) Faith is often a key element in receiving what God offers.

5. c) It involves believing in things that aren't yet tangible.

True or False

6. False

7. False

8. True

9. False

10. False

Fill in the Blank

11. faith

12. east

13. before

14. faith

15. faith

Who Said That?

16. b) Paul (or the author of Hebrews)

17. c) The father of a demon-possessed boy

Bible Book Breakdown

18. Genesis

19. Hebrews

Subsection 4: Hope & Perseverance

The Bible has several examples of people who faced impossible odds and didn't give up, all because of hope and perseverance. This section is all about how faith helps us push through.

Multiple Choice Missions

1. Which Old-Testament prophet said, "Though a righteous man falls seven times, he rises again"?

    a) Jeremiah

    b) Micah

    c) Isaiah

    d) Solomon

2. When Paul and Silas were thrown into prison, what did they do at midnight?

    a) Slept

    b) Complained

    c) Sang hymns and prayed

    d) Planned an escape

3. Who urged the Israelites, "Be strong and courageous... the LORD himself goes before you"?

    a) Joshua

    b) Moses

    c) Caleb

    d) Samuel

4. Which New-Testament letter pictures hope as "an anchor for the soul"?

    a) James

    b) 1 Peter

    c) Hebrews

    d) Jude

5. The woman who touched Jesus' cloak had been sick for how many years?

    a) 7

    b) 10

    c) 12

    d) 38

True or False:

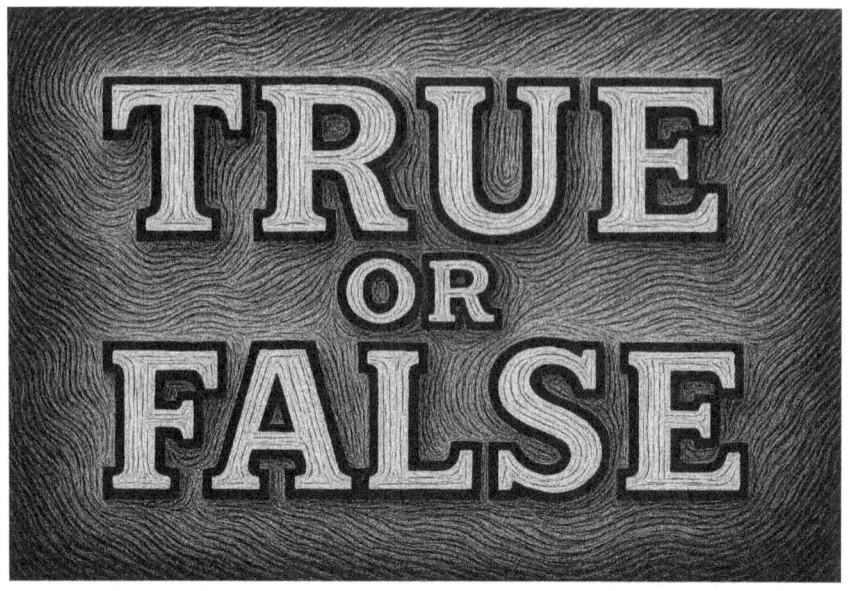

6. True or False: Job's friends immediately comforted him without judging him.

7. True or False: Noah is described as "blameless" in his generation.

8. True or False: Jeremiah quit preaching after being mocked.

9. True or False: Ruth persevered in caring for Naomi even when it meant gleaning leftovers.

10. True or False: Paul compared the Christian life to running a race that requires endurance.

Fill in the Blank:

11. "Those who hope in the LORD will renew their _____."

12. While in the lions' den, the lions' mouths were shut by _____.

13. Jesus told a parable of a persistent _____ who kept asking a judge for justice.

14. In Revelation, the church at Smyrna is encouraged to be faithful even to the point of _____.

15. Hebrews says we are surrounded by a great cloud of _____.

Who Said That?

16. "Even if he slays me, yet will I hope in him."

    a) David

    b) Job

    c) Hezekiah

    d) Habakkuk

17. "I have fought the good fight, I have finished the race, I have kept the faith."

    a) Peter

    b) Paul

    c) John

    d) Stephen

Bible Book Breakdown

18. Habakkuk's dialogue of questions and hope is in the book of _____.

19. The prison-worship episode of Paul and Silas appears in the book of _____.

Answers

Multiple Choice Missions

1. d) Solomon

2. c) Sang hymns and prayed

3. a) Joshua

4. c) Hebrews

5. c) 12

True or False

6. False

7. True

8. False

9. True

10. True

Fill in the Blank

11. strength

12. an angel

13. Widow

14. Death

15. Witnesses

Who Said That?

16. b) Job

17. b) Paul

Bible Book Breakdown

18. Habakkuk

19. Acts

Subsection 5: Prayer & Worship

Have you ever thought about how you connect with the most important people in your life? With God, that connection is profound and transformative. This section explores prayer and worship, and how we express our reverence and adoration for Him.

Multiple Choice Missions:

1. Who wrote the line "Create in me a clean heart, O God"?

    a) Asaph

    b) David

    c) Solomon

    d) Ezra

2. Where was Jesus when the disciples asked, "Lord, teach us to pray"?

    a) Mount of Olives

    b) A synagogue

    c) A certain place, after he had been praying

    d) The Temple

3. Which king played the harp and introduced music teams for temple worship?

    a) Hezekiah

    b) Josiah

    c) David

    d) Jehoshaphat

4. Hannah's heartfelt prayer for a son is in which book?

    a) Ruth

    b) 1 Samuel

    c) Judges

    d) 2 Kings

5. Who thanked God three times a day facing Jerusalem, even under threat of death?

    a) Nehemiah

    b) Daniel

    c) Mordecai

    d) Ezra

True or False:

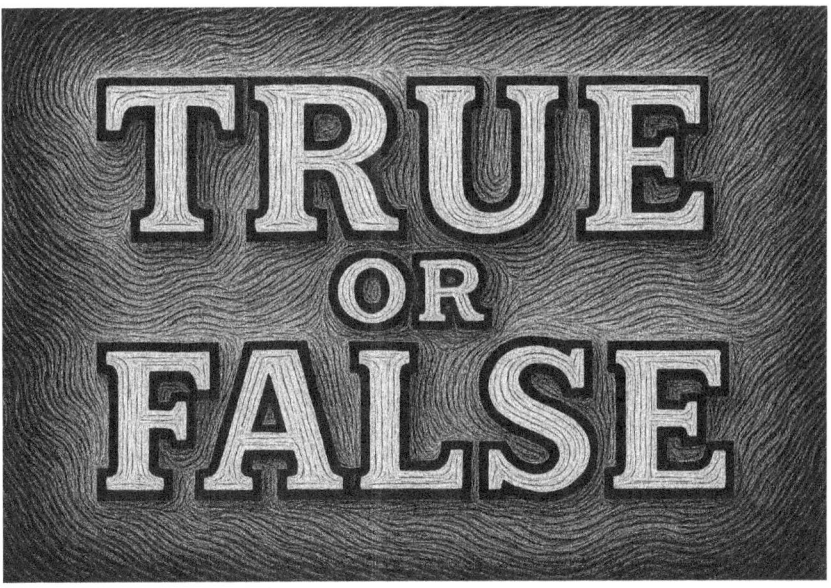

6. True or False: Jesus' "Lord's Prayer" is found only in Matthew.

7. True or False: Paul instructs believers to "pray without ceasing."

8. True or False: Miriam led Israel in worship with a tambourine after crossing the Red Sea.

9. True or False: The Psalms were Israel's primary songbook of worship.

10. True or False: Only priests were allowed to pray in Old-Testament times.

Fill in the Blank:

11. "Enter his gates with _____ and his courts with praise."

12. Jesus said, "True worshipers will worship the Father in spirit and in _____."

13. The early church "devoted themselves to the apostles' teaching and to _____."

14. Paul and Silas were praying in the prison at the city of _____.

15. Psalm 150 ends with "Let everything that has _____ praise the LORD."

Who Said That?

16. "Speak, LORD, for your servant is listening."

   a) Samuel

   b) Solomon

   c) Elisha

   d) Gideon

17. "Bless the LORD, O my soul, and forget not all his benefits."

   a) Moses

   b) David

   c) Isaiah

   d) Jonah

Bible Book Breakdown:

18. Jesus' high-priestly prayer for his disciples is in John chapter
   _____.

19. Paul's hymn about Christ emptying himself appears in the book
   of _____ (chapter 2).

Answers

Multiple Choice Missions

1. b) David

2. c) A certain place, after he had been praying

3. c) David

4. b) 1 Samuel

5. b) Daniel

True or False

6. False

7. True

8. True

9. True

10. False

Fill in the Blank

11. Thanksgiving

12. Truth

13. fellowship/prayer

14. Philippi

15. breath

Who Said That?

16. a) Samuel

17. b) David

Bible Breakdown

18. 17

19. Philippian

Subsection 6: Wisdom & Guidance

God's Word is packed with wisdom to help you navigate life. This section is all about finding that divine direction and making smart moves for your life.

Multiple Choice Missions:

1. Which book personifies Wisdom as a woman calling out in the streets?

    a) Job

    b) Ecclesiastes

    c) Proverbs

    d) Psalms

2. Solomon asked God for what gift when he became king?

    a) Riches

    b) Long life

    c) Wisdom

    d) Military power

3. Which NT epistle says, "If any of you lacks wisdom, you should ask God"?

    a) 1 Peter

    b) James

    c) Hebrews

    d) Jude

4. Who advised Moses to appoint helpers to judge smaller cases?

    a) Aaron

    b) Jethro

    c) Joshua

    d) Caleb

5. The phrase "Fear of the LORD is the beginning of knowledge" appears first in which chapter?

    a) Proverbs 1

    b) Psalm 1

    c) Job 28

    d) Ecclesiastes 12

True or False:

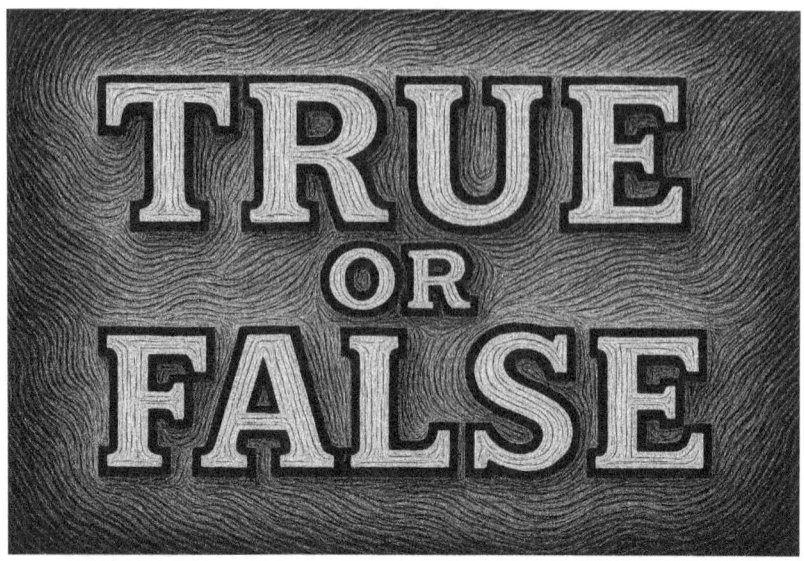

6. True or False: The book of James compares doubting to a wave of the sea blown and tossed by the wind.

7. True or False: Ecclesiastes concludes that everything is meaningless, full stop, with no hope.

8. True or False: Gideon sought guidance by placing a fleece of wool on the ground.

9. True or False: Jesus told a parable about wise and foolish builders to teach about obedience.

10. True or False: Paul relied only on visions for guidance, never on advice from believers.

Fill in the Blank:

11. "Your word is a lamp to my _____ and a light for my path."

12. Proverbs warns, "Trust in the LORD with all your heart and lean not on your own _____."

13. Isaiah promises, "Whether you turn to the right or to the left, you will hear a voice saying, 'This is the _____; walk in it.'"

14. Jesus told Martha that only one thing was needed, and _____ had chosen it.

15. The Urim and _____ were priestly tools used to discern God's will.

Who Said That?

16. "Give your servant a discerning heart to govern your people."
    a) David
    b) Solomon
    c) Hezekiah
    d) Josiah

17. "I will instruct you and teach you in the way you should go."
    a) God in Psalm 32
    b) Moses
    c) Elijah
    d) Paul

Bible Book Breakdown:

18. The famous "fleece test" of Gideon appears in the book of
    _____.

19. Proverbs 31's acrostic poem praises a wife of _____
    character.

Answers

Multiple Choice Missions

1. c) Proverbs

2. c) Wisdom

3. b) James

4. b) Jethro

5. a) Proverbs 1

True or False

6. True

7. False

8. True

9. True

10. False

Fill in the Blank

11. Feet

12. Understanding

13. Way

14. Mary

15. Thummim

Who Said That?

16. b) Solomon

17. a) God in Psalm 32

Bible Book Breakdown

18. Judges

19. noble/excellent

Subsection 7: Justice & Mercy

Have you ever been in a situation where something just didn't feel fair? Or maybe you messed up and desperately hoped for a second chance? That's exactly what this section is about: God's heart for justice and His incredible mercy. Let's take a closer look at how God stands for what's right and also how He extends amazing grace.

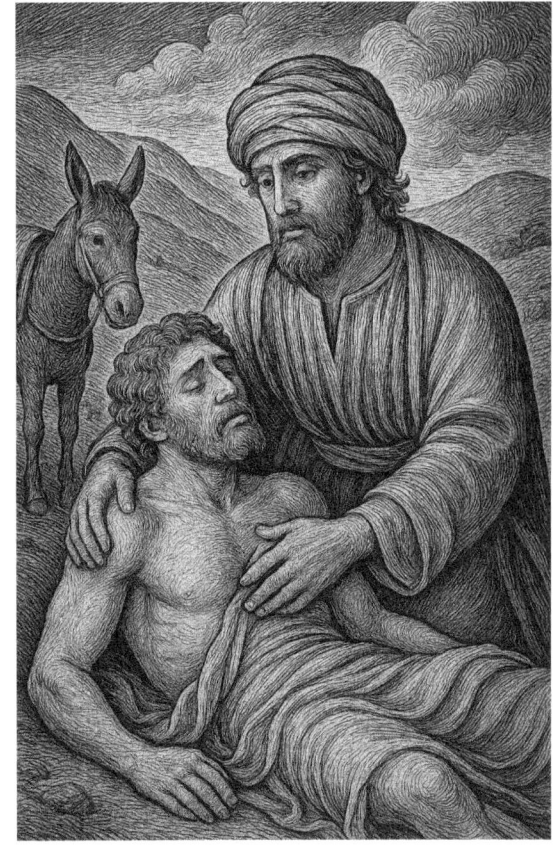

Multiple Choice Missions:

1. Which prophet declared, "Let justice roll on like a river"?

    a) Joel

    b) Amos

    c) Micah

    d) Hosea

2. Jesus illustrated neighbor-love with the parable of the _____ Samaritan.

    a) Caring

    b) Good

    c) Generous

    d) Great

3. Which Old-Testament law ensured the poor could gather leftover crops?

    a) Tithing

    b) Gleaning

    c) Jubilee

    d) Cities of refuge

4. Micah 6:8 says God requires us to act justly, love mercy, and walk _____ with him.

    a) Boldly

    b) Humbly

    c) Quickly

    d) Perfectly

5. Who pleaded for Sodom, asking if God would spare the city for ten righteous people?

    a) Lot

    b) Abraham

    c) Jacob

    d) Isaac

True or False:

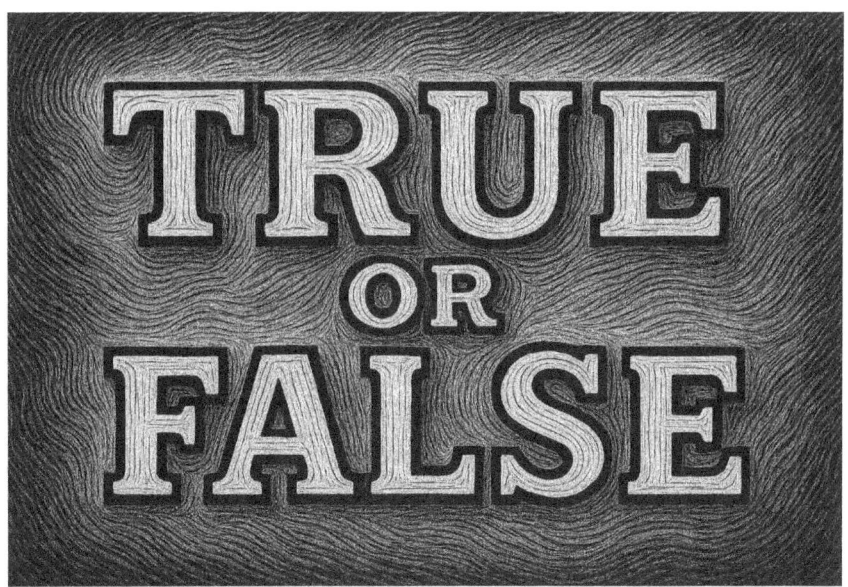

6. True or False: The Year of Jubilee canceled debts and returned land every 50 years.

7. True or False: Jonah was excited when God forgave Nineveh.

8. True or False: Jesus stopped a crowd from stoning a woman by writing on the ground.

9. True or False: Isaiah calls God a "God of justice."

10. True or False: Zacchaeus promised to repay those he cheated four times the amount.

Fill in the Blank:

11. Proverbs says, "Speak up for those who cannot _____ for themselves."

12. Jesus taught, "Blessed are the _____, for they will be shown mercy."

13. God told Israel, "Do not mistreat or oppress a _____, for you were _____ in Egypt."

14. The prophet Nathan confronted King _____ for his injustice toward Uriah.

15. Jesus quoted Hosea: "I desire mercy, not _____."

Who Said That?

16. "You intended to harm me, but God intended it for good."

    a) Joseph

    b) Moses

    c) Samuel

    d) Ezra

17. "Will not the Judge of all the earth do right?"

    a) Abraham

    b) Job

    c) David

    d) Habakkuk

Bible Book Breakdown:

18. The parable of the Good Samaritan appears in the Gospel of _____ (chapter 10).

19. Amos's justice-river quote is in Amos chapter _____.

Answers

Multiple Choice Missions

1. b) Amos

2. b) Good

3. b) Gleaning

4. b) Humbly

5. a) Abraham

True or False

6. True

7. False

8. True

9. True

10. True

Fill in the Blank

11. Speak

12. Merciful

13. foreigner/alien/stranger, foreigners/aliens/strangers

14. David

15. Sacrifice

Who Said That?

16. a) Joseph

17. a) Abraham

Bible Book Breakdown

18. Luke

19. 5

Subsection 8: Courage & Risk-Taking

Ever felt that knot in your stomach when you know you need to do something tough or step way out of your comfort zone? Many ordinary people in the Bible showed courage and took huge risks, not for fame, but for God.

Multiple Choice Missions:

1. Esther risked her life by approaching King _____ without being summoned.

    a) Nebuchadnezzar

    b) Ahasuerus/Xerxes

    c) Artaxerxes

    d) Darius

2. Which disciple leapt out of the boat to walk on water toward Jesus?

    a) Andrew

    b) Peter

    c) John

    d) Philip

3. Shadrach, Meshach, and Abednego stood up to worship a golden image under which king?

    a) Darius

    b) Belshazzar

    c) Nebuchadnezzar

    d) Cyrus

4. What young prophet confronted King David with a story about a stolen lamb?

    a) Gad

    b) Ahijah

    c) Nathan

    d) Samuel

5. Who hid the Israelite spies on Jericho's wall?

    a) Deborah

    b) Rahab

    c) Leah

    d) Miriam

True or False:

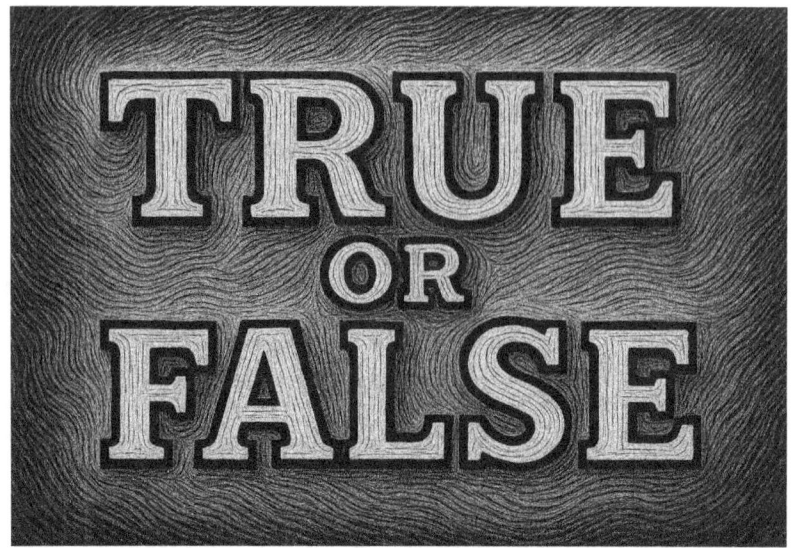

6. True or False: Jesus told Jairus, "Don't be afraid; just believe."

7. True or False: Gideon's first act of courage was destroying his father's Baal altar at night.

8. True or False: Stephen's bold sermon led directly to his immediate release.

9. True or False: Barnabas risked his reputation by introducing Saul/Paul to the Jerusalem church.

10. True or False: Moses first refused God's call because he feared public speaking.

Fill in the Blank:

11. The angel told Mary, "Do not be afraid, you have found _____ with God."

12. David told Goliath, "You come against me with sword and spear, but I come against you in the name of the _____ of Hosts."

13. After healing the lame man, Peter declared, "We must obey _____ rather than men."

14. Jonathan and his armor-bearer said, "Nothing can hinder the LORD from saving, whether by many or by _____."

15. Hebrews urges believers to "approach God's throne of grace with _____."

Who Said That?

16. "Perhaps you have come to your royal position for such a time as this."

    a) Mordecai

    b) Haman

    c) Ezra

    d) Nehemiah

17. "Here am I. Send me!"

    a) Jeremiah

    b) Isaiah

    c) Ezekiel

    d) Elisha

Bible Book Breakdown:

18. Daniel's fiery-furnace story is in Daniel chapter _____.

19. Rahab's brave hiding mission shows up in the book of _____ (chapter 2).

Answers

Multiple Choice Missions

1. b) Ahasuerus/Xerxes

2. b) Peter

3. c) Nebuchadnezzar

4. c) Nathan

5. b) Rahab

True or False

6. True

7. True

8. False

9. True

10. True

Fill in the Blank

11. Favor

12. Lord

13. God

14. Few

15. confidence/boldness

Who Said That?

16. a) Mordecai

17. b) Isaiah

Bible Book Breakdown

18. 3

19. Joshua

Section 4 – Lightning Round
(100 Rapid-Fire Questions)
(All multiple-choice; keep them quick!)

Have you been enjoying the quiz sections so far? Now, let's level up the challenge in the next couple of sections! Once you've written down your answers, you can scroll to the end of this book to get the answers.

1. The "abomination of desolation" phrase in Daniel 9 is quoted by Jesus in which chapter?

    a) Matthew 24

    b) Luke 21

    c) John 17

    d) Mark 11

2. Which Minor Prophet is almost identical in content to parts of Jeremiah?

    a) Nahum

    b) Obadiah

    c) Habakkuk

    d) Zephaniah

3. John's seven signs include turning water to wine and which final sign before the cross?

    a) Walking on water

    b) Raising Lazarus

    c) Feeding 5 000

    d) Healing blind man

4. Who served as governor of Judah during the rebuilding of the temple (Haggai 1)?

    a) Ezra

    b) Nehemiah

    c) Zerubbabel

    d) Sheshbazzar

5. Paul's "hymn of love" (agapē) appears in which chapter?

    a) Romans 8

    b) 1 Cor 13

    c) Eph 3

    d) Phil 2

6. Tribe that supplied Israel's line of priests?

    a) Judah

    b) Levi

    c) Benjamin

    d) Dan

7. Jesus healed ten lepers; how many returned to thank him?

    a) 1

    b) 3

    c) 5

    d) 10

8. King who found the Book of the Law during temple repairs?

    a) Hezekiah

    b) Josiah

    c) Jehoram

    d) Uzziah

9. Which letter mentions Melchizedek the most?

    a) Galatians

    b) Hebrews

    c) 1 Peter

    d) Colossians

10. What was the name of the city where disciples were first called "Christians"?

    a) Jerusalem

    b) Antioch

    c) Ephesus

    d) Corinth

11. Who was Israel's longest-reigning king?

    a) Manasseh

    b) David

    c) Hezekiah

    d) Zedekiah

12. Which gospel is shortest?

    a) Matthew

    b) Mark

    c) Luke

    d) John

13. What bird did Noah release second?

    a) Dove

    b) Raven

    c) Sparrow

    d) Eagle

14. Paul was shipwrecked on which island?

    a) Crete

    b) Malta

    c) Cyprus

    d) Patmos

15. How many chapters are in Psalms?

    a) 100

    b) 119

    c) 150

    d) 180

16. Who dreamed of a statue with four metals?

    a) Daniel

    b) Nebuchadnezzar

    c) Joseph

    d) Belshazzar

17. First miracle of Jesus?

    a) Walking on water

    b) Water to wine

    c) Healing leper

    d) Feeding 5 000

18. Book that ends "Grace be with all."

    a) Revelation

    b) Jude

    c) Philemon

    d) 3 John

19. Prophet who saw wheels within wheels?
    a) Isaiah
    b) Ezekiel
    c) Zechariah
    d) Malachi

20. How many spies did Moses send?
    a) 10
    b) 12
    c) 2
    d) 70

21. Jesus wept over which city?
    a) Bethany
    b) Jerusalem
    c) Capernaum
    d) Nazareth

22. Who was Moses' sister?
    a) Zipporah
    b) Miriam
    c) Hannah
    d) Deborah

23. The Beatitudes open which sermon?
    a) Mount
    b) Plain
    c) Temple
    d) Seaside

24. Oldest man in the Bible?
    a) Adam
    b) Seth
    c) Enoch
    d) Methuselah

25. Jacob's favorite son?

a) Reuben

b) Joseph

c) Benjamin

d) Judah

26. First Christian martyr?

a) James

b) Stephen

c) Peter

d) Paul

27. Plague #9 in Egypt?

a) Frogs

b) Locusts

c) Darkness

d) Hail

28. King with a writing on the wall?

a) Belshazzar

b) Darius

c) Xerxes

d) Ahab

29. Jesus' foster father's trade?

a) Fisherman

b) Carpenter

c) Farmer

d) Scribe

30. River Jordan parted for which prophet's cloak?

a) Samuel

b) Elisha

c) Jeremiah

d) Obadiah

31. Which judge of Israel was also a prophetess?

    a) Ruth

    b) Deborah

    c) Esther

    d) Jael

32. What was the name of the mountain where the Law was given to Moses?

    a) Mount Zion

    b) Mount Sinai

    c) Mount Carmel

    d) Mount of Olives

33. In the New Testament, who raised Tabitha (Dorcas) from the dead?

    a) Peter

    b) Paul

    c) John

    d) Luke

34. Which book of the Old Testament is a collection of love poems?

    a) Proverbs

    b) Ecclesiastes

    c) Song of Songs

    d) Lamentations

35. What was the name of the sorcerer who opposed Paul in Paphos?

    a) Simon Magus

    b) Bar-Jesus (Elymas)

    c) Apollos

    d) Barnabas

36. How many baskets of leftover food were collected after Jesus fed the 5,000?

    a) Seven

    b) Twelve

    c) Five

    d) Ten

37. Which Old Testament prophet is known for his visions of the end times, similar to Revelation?

    a) Amos

    b) Hosea

    c) Daniel

    d) Micah

38. What was the name of the garden where Jesus prayed before his crucifixion?

    a) Garden of Eden

    b) Garden of Gethsemane

    c) Mount of Olives

    d) Bethany

39. Who was the first Gentile convert recorded in the book of Acts?

    a) Lydia

    b) Cornelius

    c) Silas

    d) Timothy

40. Which book of the Old Testament expresses deep sorrow over the destruction of Jerusalem?

    a) Ezekiel

    b) Jeremiah

    c) Lamentations

    d) Habakkuk

41. What was the name of the angel who announced Jesus' birth to Mary?

    a) Michael

    b) Gabriel

    c) Raphael

    d) Uriel

42. Which of Paul's letters is addressed to the churches in Galatia?

    a) Philippians

    b) Ephesians

    c) Galatians

    d) Colossians

43. What was the occupation of Zacchaeus, whom Jesus called down from a tree?

   a) Fisherman

   b) Tax collector

   c) Carpenter

   d) Shepherd

44. Which Old Testament book contains the story of Shadrach, Meshach, and Abednego in the fiery furnace?

   a) Isaiah

   b) Jeremiah

   c) Daniel

   d) Ezekiel

45. What was the name of the first king of the divided kingdom of Israel (the northern kingdom)?

   a) Rehoboam

   b) Jeroboam

   c) Ahab

   d) Hoshea

46. Which book of the New Testament is a letter written by the brother of Jesus?

   a) 1 Peter

   b) 2 Peter

   c) James

   d) Jude

47. What was the name of the well where Jesus spoke to the Samaritan woman?

   a) Well of Abraham

   b) Jacob's Well

   c) Well of Isaac

   d) Well of Rebekah

48. Which Old Testament prophet used the analogy of a potter and clay to describe God's sovereignty?

    a) Isaiah

    b) Jeremiah

    c) Ezekiel

    d) Hosea

49. What was the name of the Roman centurion who declared, "Surely this man was the Son of God!"?

    a) Cornelius

    b) Longinus

    c) Julius

    d) Festus

50. Which book of the Old Testament is a collection of wisdom literature that questions the meaning of life?

    a) Proverbs

    b) Job

    c) Ecclesiastes

    d) Psalms

51. What was the name of Saul's general?

    a) Joab

    b) Abner

    c) Benaiah

    d) Adonijah

52. In what town did Jesus grow up?

    a) Bethlehem

    b) Nazareth

    c) Capernaum

    d) Jerusalem

53. Which of the following was NOT one of the gifts brought to the infant Jesus by the Magi?

    a) Gold

    b) Frankincense

    c) Myrrh

    d) Silver

54. What was the name of the short tax collector who climbed a sycamore-fig tree to see Jesus?

   a) Matthew

   b) Zacchaeus

   c) Levi

   d) Barnabas

55. Which Old Testament prophet was a shepherd and a fig-tree dresser?

   a) Amos

   b) Micah

   c) Hosea

   d) Joel

56. On what mountain did the transfiguration of Jesus occur?

   a) Mount Sinai

   b) Mount Hermon

   c) Mount Tabor

   d) Mount of Olives

57. Who was the Roman governor who presided over Paul's trial in Caesarea?

   a) Pontius Pilate

   b) Felix

   c) Festus

   d) Agrippa

58. What was the name of Abraham's nephew?

   a) Isaac

   b) Jacob

   c) Lot

   d) Ishmael

59. Which book of the Old Testament is a series of prophetic visions concerning the rebuilding of the temple and the coming Messiah?

   a) Haggai

   b) Zechariah

   c) Malachi

   d) Joel

60. What was the name of the pool in Jerusalem where Jesus healed a paralyzed man who had been lying there for 38 years?

    a) Pool of Siloam

    b) Pool of Bethesda

    c) Gihon Spring

    d) King's Pool

61. Who was the first wife of Jacob?

    a) Rachel

    b) Leah

    c) Bilhah

    d) Zilpah

62. Which of the following was NOT one of the signs given by Jesus in the Olivet Discourse concerning the end times?

    a) Wars and rumors of wars

    b) Famines and earthquakes

    c) A prolonged period of worldwide peace

    d) Persecution of believers

63. What was the name of the angel who appeared to Zechariah to announce the birth of John the Baptist?

    a) Michael

    b) Gabriel

    c) Raphael

    d) Uriel

64. Which book of the Old Testament contains the story of the writing on the wall during Belshazzar's feast?

    a) Ezekiel

    b) Daniel

    c) Isaiah

    d) Jeremiah

65. Who was the successor to the prophet Elijah?

    a) Elisha

    b) Micaiah

    c) Obadiah

    d) Habakkuk

66. What was the name of the town where Jesus performed his first miracle of turning water into wine?

a) Bethany

b) Cana

c) Capernaum

d) Nain

67. Which of Paul's letters was written to a church in a city famous for its temple dedicated to Artemis (Diana)?

a) Philippians

b) Colossians

c) Ephesians

d) 1 Thessalonians

68. What was the name of Isaac's wife?

a) Sarah

b) Rebekah

c) Rachel

d) Leah

69. Which of the following is NOT one of the major prophets in the Old Testament?

a) Isaiah

b) Jeremiah

c) Ezekiel

d) Amos

70. What was the name of the high priest who questioned Peter and John after the healing of the lame man at the temple gate?

a) Annas

b) Caiaphas

c) Gamaliel

d) Zadok

71. Who was the mother of Ishmael?

a) Sarah

b) Hagar

c) Keturah

d) Rebekah

72. Which of the following was NOT one of the temptations Jesus faced in the wilderness?

   a) Turning stones into bread

   b) Throwing himself down from the temple

   c) Being offered all the kingdoms of the world

   d) Being tempted to call down fire from heaven

73. What was the name of the Roman governor who interrogated Jesus before Pontius Pilate?

   a) Herod Agrippa I

   b) Herod Antipas

   c) Felix

   d) Festus

74. Which book of the Old Testament contains the story of Queen Vashti and Esther?

   a) Ruth

   b) Esther

   c) Nehemiah

   d) Ezra

75. Who was the disciple who replaced Judas Iscariot?

   a) Barnabas

   b) Silas

   c) Matthias

   d) Luke

76. What was the name of the town where Lazarus, Mary, and Martha lived?

   a) Bethany

   b) Capernaum

   c) Jericho

   d) Nain

77. Which of Paul's letters addresses issues of spiritual gifts and the resurrection?

    a) Philippians

    b) 2 Corinthians

    c) 1 Corinthians

    d) Ephesians

78. Who was the father of King David?

    a) Jesse

    b) Saul

    c) Jonathan

    d) Samuel

79. Which of the following is NOT one of the pastoral epistles?

    a) 1 Timothy

    b) 2 Timothy

    c) Titus

    d) Philemon

80. What was the name of the Sanhedrin member who provided his own tomb for Jesus' burial?

    a) Nicodemus

    b) Joseph of Arimathea

    c) Lazarus

    d) Zacchaeus

81. Who was the wife of Isaac?

    a) Sarah

    b) Rebekah

    c) Rachel

    d) Leah

82. Which of the following was NOT one of the miracles performed by Elisha?

    a) Raising a widow's son

    b) Healing Naaman's leprosy

    c) Turning water into wine

    d) Multiplying a widow's oil

83. What was the name of the proconsul of Cyprus who was converted after hearing Paul and Barnabas?

  a) Sergius Paulus

  b) Gallio

  c) Lysanias

  d) Erastus

84. Which book of the Old Testament contains the prophecies of Habakkuk?

  a) Amos

  b) Hosea

  c) Habakkuk

  d) Zephaniah

85. Who was the disciple who was a physician?

  a) Peter

  b) John

  c) Luke

  d) Matthew

86. What was the name of the town where Jesus raised a widow's son from the dead?

  a) Bethany

  b) Cana

  c) Capernaum

  d) Nain

87. Which of Paul's letters was written to a church in a city known for its philosophical schools?

  a) Philippians

  b) Colossians

  c) Thessalonica

  d) Corinth

88. Who was the father of John the Baptist?

  a) Zechariah

  b) Simeon

  c) Joseph

  d) Joachim

89. Which of the following is NOT one of the prison epistles?

   a) Ephesians

   b) Philippians

   c) Colossians

   d) 1 Thessalonians

90. What was the name of the high priest who questioned Jesus before the Sanhedrin along with Caiaphas?

   a) Annas

   b) Gamaliel

   c) Zadok

   d) Abiathar

91. Who was the mother of Jacob and Esau?

   a) Sarah

   b) Rebekah

   c) Rachel

   d) Leah

92. Which of the following was NOT one of the signs that occurred at Jesus' crucifixion?

   a) Darkness over the land

   b) An earthquake

   c) The tearing of the temple curtain

   d) A great storm at sea

93. What was the name of the governor who succeeded Felix in Judea and heard Paul's defense?

   a) Pontius Pilate

   b) Herod Agrippa II

   c) Festus

   d) Claudius Lysias

94. Which book of the Old Testament contains the prophecies of Haggai?

   a) Zechariah

   b) Malachi

   c) Haggai

   d) Obadiah

95. Who was the disciple who was a tax collector?

    a) Peter

    b) James

    c) Matthew

    d) John

96. What was the name of the town where the Apostle Paul was stoned and left for dead during his first missionary journey?

    a) Lystra

    b) Iconium

    c) Antioch of Pisidia

    d) Derbe

97. Which book of the Old Testament contains the prophecies of Malachi?

    a) Zechariah

    b) Haggai

    c) Malachi

    d) Joel

98. Who was the disciple who was known as "the one whom Jesus loved"?

    a) Peter

    b) James

    c) John

    d) Andrew

99. What was the name of the island to which the Apostle John was exiled when he wrote the book of Revelation?

    a) Malta

    b) Cyprus

    c) Patmos

    d) Crete

100. Which of the following Old Testament books is primarily a collection of wisdom sayings attributed to King Solomon?

    a) Ecclesiastes

    b) Job

    c) Proverbs

    d) Song of Songs

Answers

1. a) Matthew 24
2. b) Obadiah
3. b) Raising Lazarus
4. c) Zerubbabel
5. b) 1 Cor 13
6. b) Levi
7. a) 1
8. b) Josiah
9. b) Hebrews
10. b) Antioch
11. a) Manasseh
12. b) Mark
13. a) Dove
14. b) Malta
15. c) 150
16. b) Nebuchadnezzar
17. b) Water to wine
18. d) 3 John
19. b) Ezekiel
20. b) 12
21. b) Jerusalem
22. b) Miriam
23. a) Mount
24. d) Methuselah
25. b) Joseph
26. b) Stephen
27. c) Darkness
28. a) Belshazzar
29. b) Carpenter
30. b) Elisha
31. b) Deborah

52. b) Nazareth
53. d) Silver
54. b) Zacchaeus
55. a) Amos
56. c) Mount Tabor
57. b) Felix
58. c) Lot
59. b) Zechariah
60. b) Pool of Bethesda
61. b) Leah
62. c) A prolonged period of worldwide peace
63. b) Gabriel
64. b) Daniel
65. a) Elisha
66. b) Cana
67. c) Ephesians
68. b) Rebekah
69. d) Amos
70. a) Annas
71. b) Hagar
72. d) Being tempted to call down fire from heaven
73. b) Herod Antipas
74. b) Esther
75. c) Matthias
76. a) Bethany
77. c) 1 Corinthians
78. a) Jesse
79. d) Philemon
80. b) Joseph of Arimathea

32. b) Mount Sinai

33. a) Peter

34. c) Song of Songs

35. b) Bar-Jesus (Elymas)

36. b) Twelve

37. c) Daniel

38. b) Garden of Gethsemane

39. b) Cornelius

40. c) Lamentations

41. b) Gabriel

42. c) Galatians

43. b) Tax collector

44. c) Daniel

45. b) Jeroboam

46. c) James

47. b) Jacob's Well

48. b) Jeremiah

49. b) Longinus

50. c) Ecclesiastes

51. b) Abner

81. b) Rebekah

82. c) Turning water into wine

83. a) Sergius Paulus

84. c) Habakkuk

85. c) Luke

86. d) Nain

87. d) Corinth

88. a) Zechariah

89. d) 1 Thessalonians

90. a) Annas

91. b) Rebekah

92. d) A great storm at sea

93. c) Festus

94. c) Haggai

95. c) Matthew

96. a) Lystra

97. c) Malachi

98. c) John

99. c) Patmos

100. c) Proverbs

Section 5 – Ultimate Challenge

50 Fill in the Blank

1. "Man shall not live on _____ alone, but on every word that comes from the mouth of God."

2. After Elijah, _____ asked for a double portion of his spirit.

3. "Perfect love casts out _____."

4. The fruit of the Spirit listed in Galatians starts with "love, joy, _____."

5. Moses' face shone after he spoke with _____.

6. The shortest verse in English language Bibles: "Jesus _____."

7. The armor of God includes the breastplate of _____.

8. Revelation's final invitation says, "Let the one who is _____ come."

9. The Great Commission ends with "I am with you _____."

10. Rahab tied a _____ cord in her window.

11. "I have been crucified with Christ and I no longer live, but _____ lives in me."

12. Before becoming Paul, he was known by his Hebrew name, _____.

13. "For the wages of sin is _____ , but the gift of God is eternal life in Christ Jesus our Lord."

14. The Passover meal commemorates the Israelites' deliverance from slavery in _____.

15. The Old Testament prophet _____ had visions of a valley of dry bones.

16. "For where two or three gather in my name, there _____ I am with them."

17. The Apostle _____ wrote the book of Revelation while exiled on the island of Patmos.

18. The Old Testament book of _____ is a collection of wise sayings.

19. "Blessed are the _____ , for they will be comforted." (Matthew 5:4)

20. The city of _____ was destroyed by fire and brimstone because of its wickedness.

21. "The Lord is my shepherd; I shall not _____ ."

22. The Apostle _____ initially doubted Jesus' resurrection.

23. The Old Testament book of _____ tells the story of a man who lost everything but remained faithful to God.

24. "For all have sinned and fall short of the _____ of God."

25. The first miracle performed by the Apostle Peter after Pentecost was healing a lame man at the Beautiful Gate of the temple in _____.

26. "For God did not send his Son into the world to _____ the world, but to save the world through him."

27. The Old Testament prophet _____ challenged the prophets of Baal on Mount Carmel.

28. "_____ the Lord, all you nations; extol him, all you peoples." (Psalm 117:1)

29. The Apostle _____ wrote several letters, including those to the churches in Corinth.

30. The parable of the _____ and the tax collector highlights the importance of humility in prayer.

31. "The _____ of the Lord is the beginning of wisdom." (Psalm 111:10)

32. The Apostle _____ wrote the Gospel that emphasizes Jesus' divine nature.

33. The Old Testament book of _____ contains songs of worship and praise.

34. "For by grace you have been saved, through _____ —and this is not from yourselves, it is the gift of God."

35. The early Christian deacon _____ was stoned for his faith.

36. "I can do all things through _____ who strengthens me." (Philippians 4:13)

37. The Old Testament prophet _____ foretold the coming of a messenger who would prepare the way for the Lord.

38. "The steadfast love of the Lord never ceases; his _____ never come to an end." (Lamentations 3:22)

39. The Apostle _____ wrote letters that address issues of social justice and the rich and poor.

40. The parable of the _____ Seed illustrates the growth of the Kingdom of God.

41. "_____ to the Lord, for he is good; his love endures forever." (1 Chronicles 16:34)

42. The Apostle _____ was the brother of Jesus and wrote a letter emphasizing practical faith.

43. The Old Testament book of _____ tells the story of a prophet who was swallowed by a large fish.

44. "For where your _____ is, there your heart will be also." (Matthew 6:21)

45. The early Christian couple _____ and Priscilla were close associates of Paul.

46. "Be _____ in hope, patient in affliction, faithful in prayer." (Romans 12:12)

47. The Old Testament prophet _____ confronted King David about his sin with Bathsheba.

48. "The Lord bless you and _____ you; the Lord make his face shine on you and be gracious to you." (Numbers 6:24-25)

49. The Apostle _____ wrote letters that warn against false teachers and emphasize the importance of love.

50. The parable of the _____ Servant teaches about the importance of forgiveness.

Answers

1. "Man shall not live on **bread** alone, but on every word that comes from the mouth of God."

2. After Elijah, **Elisha** asked for a double portion of his spirit.

3. "Perfect love casts out **fear**."

4. The fruit of the Spirit listed in Galatians starts with "love, joy, **peace**."

5. Moses' face shone after he spoke with **God**.

6. The shortest verse in English Bibles: "Jesus **wept**."

7. The armor of God includes the breastplate of **righteousness**.

8. Revelation's final invitation says, "Let the one who is **thirsty** come."

9. The Great Commission ends with "I am with you **always**."

10. Rahab tied a **scarlet** cord in her window.

11. "I have been crucified with Christ and I no longer live, but **Christ** lives in me."

12. Before becoming Paul, he was known by his Hebrew name, **Saul**.

13. "For the wages of sin is **death**, but the gift of God is eternal life in Christ Jesus our Lord."

14. The Passover meal commemorates the Israelites' deliverance from slavery in **Egypt**.

15. The Old Testament prophet **Ezekiel** had visions of a valley of dry bones.

16. "For where two or three gather in my name, there **I** am with them."

17. The Apostle **John** wrote the book of Revelation while exiled on the island of Patmos.

18. The Old Testament book of **Proverbs** is a collection of wise sayings.

19. "Blessed are the **meek**, for they will be comforted." (Matthew 5:4)

20. The city of **Sodom** was destroyed by fire and brimstone because of its wickedness.

21. "The Lord is my shepherd; I shall not **want**."

22. The Apostle **Thomas** initially doubted Jesus' resurrection.

23. The Old Testament book of **Job** tells the story of a man who lost everything but remained faithful to God.

24. "For all have sinned and fall short of the **glory** of God."

25. The first miracle performed by the Apostle Peter after Pentecost was healing a lame man at the Beautiful Gate of the temple in **Jerusalem**.

26. "For God did not send his Son into the world to **condemn** the world, but to save the world through him."

27. The Old Testament prophet **Elijah** challenged the prophets of Baal on Mount Carmel.

28. "**Praise** the Lord, all you nations; extol him, all you peoples." (Psalm 117:1)

29. The Apostle **Paul** wrote several letters, including those to the churches in Corinth.

30. The parable of the **Pharisee** and the tax collector highlights the importance of humility in prayer.

31. "The **fear** of the Lord is the beginning of wisdom." (Psalm 111:10)

32. The Apostle **John** wrote the Gospel that emphasizes Jesus' divine nature.

33. The Old Testament book of **Psalms** contains songs of worship and praise.

34. "For by grace you have been saved, through **faith**—and this is not from yourselves, it is the gift of God."

35. The early Christian deacon **Stephen** was stoned for his faith.

36. "I can do all things through **Christ** who strengthens me." (Philippians 4:13)

37. The Old Testament prophet **Malachi** foretold the coming of a messenger who would prepare the way for the Lord.

38. "The steadfast love of the Lord never ceases; his **mercies** never come to an end." (Lamentations 3:22)

39. The Apostle **James** wrote letters that address issues of social justice and the rich and poor.

40. The parable of the **mustard** Seed illustrates the growth of the Kingdom of God.

41. "**Give thanks** to the Lord, for he is good; his love endures

forever." (1 Chronicles 16:34)

42. The Apostle **James** was the brother of Jesus and wrote a letter emphasizing practical faith.

43. The Old Testament book of **Jonah** tells the story of a prophet who was swallowed by a large fish.

44. "For where your **treasure** is, there your heart will be also." (Matthew 6:21)

45. The early Christian couple **Aquila** and Priscilla were close associates of Paul.

46. "Be **joyful** in hope, patient in affliction, faithful in prayer." (Romans 12:12)

47. The Old Testament prophet **Nathan** confronted King David about his sin with Bathsheba.

48. "The Lord bless you and **keep** you; the Lord make his face shine on you and be gracious to you." (Numbers 6:24-25)

49. The Apostle **John** wrote letters that warn against false teachers and emphasize the importance of love.

50. The parable of the **Unforgiving** Servant teaches about the importance of forgiveness.

Who Said That?

1. "My God, my God, why have you forsaken me?"

2. "Can these dry bones live?"

3. "We must obey God rather than human beings!"

4. "I am the way and the truth and the life. No one comes to the Father except through me."

5. "The spirit of the Lord is on me, because he has anointed me to proclaim good news to the poor."

6. "Where you go I will go, and where you stay I will stay. Your people will be my people and your God my God."

7. "Look, the Lamb of God, who takes away the sin of the world!"

8. "Silver or gold I do not have, but what I do have I give you. In the name of Jesus Christ of Nazareth, walk."

9. "Do not be afraid; keep on speaking, do not be silent."

10. "How long will you waver between two opinions? If the Lord is God, follow him; but if Baal is God, follow him."

11. "Unless I see the nail marks in his hands and put my finger where the nails were, and put my hand into his side, I will not believe."

12. "You are the Christ, the Son of the living God."

13. "I am not ashamed of the gospel, because it is the power of God that brings salvation to everyone who believes."

14. "Woe to me if I do not preach the gospel!"

15. "Our hearts are restless until they rest in you." (Attributed to Augustine, reflecting biblical themes)

16. "The kingdom of God is not a matter of eating and drinking, but of righteousness, peace and joy in the Holy Spirit."

17. "I have fought the good fight, I have finished the race, I have kept the faith."

18. "For everything there is a season, and a time for every matter under heaven."

19. "I know that my redeemer lives, and that in the end he will stand upon the earth."

20. "As for me and my household, we will serve the Lord."

21. "The Lord is my strength and my shield; in him my heart trusts, and I am helped; my heart exults, and with my song I give thanks to him."

Answers

1. "My God, my God, why have you forsaken me?" - **Jesus**

2. "Can these dry bones live?" - **Ezekiel**

3. "We must obey God rather than human beings!" - **Peter and the other apostles**

4. "I am the way and the truth and the life. No one comes to the Father except through me." - **Jesus**

5. "The Spirit of the Lord is on me, because he has anointed me to proclaim good news to the poor." - **Jesus**

6. "Where you go I will go, and where you stay I will stay. Your people will be my people and your God my God." - **Ruth**

7. "Look, the Lamb of God, who takes away the sin of the world!" - **John the Baptist**

8. "Silver or gold I do not have, but what I do have I give you. In the name of Jesus Christ of Nazareth, walk." - **Peter**

9. "Do not be afraid; keep on speaking, do not be silent." - **The Lord to Paul**

10. "How long will you waver between two opinions? If the Lord is God, follow him; but if Baal is God, follow him." - **Elijah**

11. "Unless I see the nail marks in his hands and put my finger where the nails were, and put my hand into his side, I will not believe." - **Thomas**

12. "You are the Christ, the Son of the living God." - **Peter**

13. "I am not ashamed of the gospel, because it is the power of God that brings salvation to everyone who believes." - **Paul**

14. "Woe to me if I do not preach the gospel!" - **Paul**

15. "Our hearts are restless until they rest in you." (Attributed to Augustine, reflecting biblical themes) - **Augustine**

16. "The kingdom of God is not a matter of eating and drinking, but of righteousness, peace and joy in the Holy Spirit." - **Paul**

17. "I have fought the good fight, I have finished the race, I have kept the faith." - **Paul**

18. "For everything there is a season, and a time for every matter under heaven." - **Solomon (Ecclesiastes)**

19. "I know that my redeemer lives, and that in the end he will stand upon the earth." - **Job**

20. "As for me and my household, we will serve the Lord." - **Joshua**

21. "The Lord is my strength and my shield; in him my heart trusts, and I am helped; my heart exults, and with my song I give thanks to him." - **David**

Extra Round: Women of the Word (50 Questions)

Part 1: Old Testament (20 Questions)

1. Who was the first woman mentioned by name in the Bible?
    a) Eve
    b) Sarah
    c) Rebekah
    d) Hagar

2. Which woman was known for her beauty and became the queen of Persia?
    a) Ruth
    b) Esther
    c) Deborah
    d) Rahab

3. Who was the mother of Samuel and prayed fervently for a child?
    a) Hannah
    b) Rachel
    c) Leah
    d) Rebekah

4. Which woman showed great loyalty to her mother-in-law Naomi?

    a) Orpah

    b) Ruth

    c) Michal

    d) Abigail

5. Who was the famous prophetess and judge?

    a) Miriam

    b) Deborah

    c) Huldah

    d) Noadiah

6. Which woman helped to save spies and her family during the fall of Jericho?

    a) Rahab

    b) Jael

    c) Delilah

    d) Rizpah

7. Who was the wife of Abraham?

    a) Hagar

    b) Keturah

    c) Sarah

    d) Milcah

8. Which woman was known for her wisdom and advised King David?

    a) Bathsheba

    b) Tamar

    c) Abigail

    d) Jezebel

9. Who was the sister of Moses and Aaron?

    a) Zipporah

    b) Elisheba

    c) Miriam

    d) Puah

10. Which woman was tricked into marrying Jacob?

   a) Rachel

   b) Leah

   c) Bilhah

   d) Zilpah

11. What was the name of Samson's mother?

   a) Zillah

   b) Manoah's wife (unnamed)

   c) Naamah

   d) Abital

12. Which woman was the wife of Isaac?

   a) Rachel

   b) Leah

   c) Rebekah

   d) Bilhah

13. Which woman was the mother of Joeph and Benjamin?

   a) Bilhah

   b) Zilpah

   c) Leah

   d) Rachel

14. Who was the only daughter of Jacob mentioned by name?

   a) Dinah

   b) Serah

   c) Asenath

   d) Jochebed

15. Which woman was the mother of Moses?

   a) Jochebed

   b) Shiprah

   c) Puah

   d) Elisheba

16. Which woman was the wife of King Ahab and known for her wickedness?

    a) Jezebel

    b) Athaliah

    c) Gomer

    d) Maacah

17. Which woman was the wife of Hosea?

    a) Gomer

    b) Rizpah

    c) Noadiah

    d) Anath

18. Which woman was known for cutting off Sisera's head with a tent peg?

    a) Deborah

    b) Jael

    c) Barak's wife (unnamed)

    d) Abishag

19. Which woman was the mother of King Solomon?

    a) Michal

    b) Bathsheba

    c) Haggith

    d) Abishag

20. Which woman was the daughter of Jephthah who mourned her virginity?

    a) Jephthah's daughter (unnamed)

    b) Iscah

    c) Milcah

    d) Maacah

Answers

1. a) Eve
2. b) Esther
3. a) Hannah
4. b) Ruth
5. b) Deborah
6. a) Rahab
7. c) Sarah
8. c) Abigail
9. c) Miriam
10. b) Leah
11. b) Manoah's wife (unnamed)
12. c) Rebekah
13. d) Rachel
14. a) Dinah
15. a) Jochebed
16. a) Jezebel
17. a) Gomer
18. b) Jael
19. b) Bathsheba
20. a) Jephthah's daughter (unnamed)

Part 2: New Testament (20 Questions)

21. Who was the mother of Jesus?

    a) Elizabeth

    b) Mary

    c) Salome

    d) Susanna

22. Which woman was the first to see Jesus after his resurrection?

    a) Mary Magdalene

    b) Mary, the mother of James

    c) Joanna

    d) Salome

23. Who was the sister of Martha and Lazarus?

    a) Mary

    b) Martha

    c) Salome

    d) Susanna

24. Which woman was known for her hospitality to Jesus?

    a) Mary Magdalene

    b) Mary, the mother of James

    c) Martha

    d) Joanna

25. Who was the mother of John the Baptist?

    a) Mary

    b) Elizabeth

    c) Anna

    d) Salome

26. Which woman was a prophetess who recognized Jesus as the Messiah in the temple?

    a) Mary

    b) Elizabeth

    c) Anna

    d) Priscilla

27. Which woman was a prominent leader in the early church and a tentmaker?

a) Lydia

b) Phoebe

c) Junia

d) Priscilla

28. Which woman was known for her generosity and hospitality in Philippi?

a) Lydia

b) Phoebe

c) Junia

d) Chloe

29. Which woman was commended by Paul as a deaconess or servant of the church?

a) Lydia

b) Phoebe

c) Junia

d) Tryphena

30. Which woman is mentioned in Romans 16 as being outstanding among the apostles?

a) Lydia

b) Phoebe

c) Junia

d) Persis

31. Who was the wife of Herod Antipas, who demanded the head of John the Baptist?

a) Joanna

b) Susanna

c) Salome

d) Herodias

32. Who was the daughter of Herodias, who danced for Herod and requested John the Baptist's head?

    a) Salome

    b) Drusilla

    c) Bernice

    d) Lydia

33. Which woman was healed by Jesus after suffering from bleeding for twelve years?

    a) Mary Magdalene

    b) Mary, the mother of James

    c) The woman with the issue of blood (unnamed)

    d) Susanna

34. Who was the wife of Zechariah and mother of John the Baptist?

    a) Mary

    b) Elizabeth

    c) Anna

    d) Salome

35. Which woman was a follower of Jesus and provided for his ministry out of her means?

    a) Mary Magdalene

    b) Joanna

    c) Susanna

    d) Mary, the mother of James

36. Which woman was the wife of Aquila and a fellow tentmaker with Paul?

    a) Phoebe

    b) Priscilla

    c) Junia

    d) Tryphena

37. Which woman is mentioned in Romans 16 as a beloved Christian worker?

 a) Persis

 b) Julia

 c) Nereus' sister (unnamed)

 d) Rufus' mother (unnamed)

38. Which woman is mentioned in Romans 16 as a chosen lady?

 a) Elect lady (unnamed)

 b) Tryphaena

 c) Tryphosa

 d) Julia

39. Which two women are mentioned in Romans 16 as workers in the Lord?

 a) Mary and Persis

 b) Tryphaena and Tryphosa

 c) Julia and Nereus' sister

 d) Rufus' mother and his sister

40. Which woman is mentioned in Romans 16 as the mother of Rufus and someone who was also a mother to Paul?

 a) Julia

 b) Tryphaena

 c) Rufus' mother (unnamed)

 d) Persis

Answers

21. b) Mary

22. a) Mary Magdalene

23. a) Mary

24. c) Martha

25. b) Elizabeth

26. c) Anna

27. d) Priscilla

28. a) Lydia

29. b) Phoebe

30. c) Junia

31. d) Herodias

32. a) Salome

33. c) The woman with the issue of blood (unnamed)

34. b) Elizabeth

35. b) Joanna

36. b) Priscilla

37. a) Persis

38. a) Elect lady (unnamed)

39. b) Tryphaena and Tryphosa

40. c) Rufus' mother (unnamed)

Part 3: Who Said That? (5 Questions)

41. "Where you go I will go, and where you stay I will stay. Your people will be my people and your God my God."

    a) Sarah

    b) Ruth

    c) Esther

    d) Hannah

42. "My soul glorifies the Lord and my spirit rejoices in God my Savior."

    a) Elizabeth

    b) Mary

    c) Anna

    d) Priscilla

43. "Do whatever he tells you."

    a) Mary (mother of Jesus)

    b) Martha

    c) Mary Magdalene

    d) Salome

44. "If I perish, I perish."

    a) Ruth

    b) Rahab

    c) Esther

    d) Jael

45. "For this child I prayed; and the Lord hath given me my petition which I asked of him"

    a) Sarah

    b) Rebekah

    c) Rachel

    d) Hannah

Answers

41. b) Ruth
42. b) Mary
43. a) Mary (mother of Jesus)
44. c) Esther
45. d) Hannah

Part 4: Fill in the Blank (5 Questions)

46. "Charm is deceptive, and beauty is fleeting; but a woman who fears the LORD is to be _____." (Proverbs 31:30, NKJV)

47. "Then God said, 'It is not good that the _____ should be alone; I will make him a helper comparable to him.' (Genesis 2:18, NKJV)

48. "And without faith it is impossible to please him, for whoever would draw near to God must believe that he exists and that he _____ those who seek him." (Hebrews 11:6, NKJV)

49. "But the fruit of the Spirit is love, joy, peace, forbearance, kindness, goodness, faithfulness, gentleness, _____." (Galatians 5:22-23, NIV)

50. "There is neither Jew nor Gentile, neither slave nor free, nor is there male and _____, for you are all one in Christ Jesus." (Galatians 3:28, NIV)

Answers

46. praised
47. man
48. rewards
49. self-control
50. woman

SCORE CARD

NAME	SECTION	SCORE

Welcome Aboard, Check Out This Limited-Time Free Bonus!

Ahoy, reader! Welcome to the Ahoy Publications family, and thanks for snagging a copy of this book! Since you've chosen to join us on this journey, we'd like to offer you something special.

Check out the link below for a FREE e-book filled with delightful facts about American History.

But that's not all - you'll also have access to our exclusive email list with even more free e-books and insider knowledge. Well, what are ye waiting for? Click the link below to join and set sail toward exciting adventures in American History.

Access your bonus here

https://ahoypublications.com/

Or, Scan the QR code!

Check out another book in the series

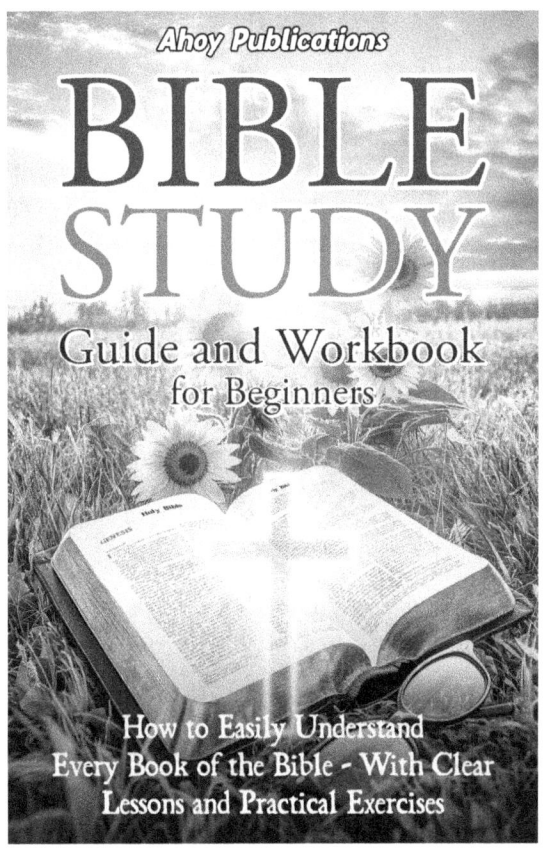

Welcome Aboard, Check Out This Limited-Time Free Bonus!

Ahoy, reader! Welcome to the Ahoy Publications family, and thanks for snagging a copy of this book! Since you've chosen to join us on this journey, we'd like to offer you something special.

Check out the link below for a FREE e-book filled with delightful facts about American History.

But that's not all - you'll also have access to our exclusive email list with even more free e-books and insider knowledge. Well, what are ye waiting for? Click the link below to join and set sail toward exciting adventures in American History.

Access your bonus here
https://ahoypublications.com/
Or, Scan the QR code!

www.ingramcontent.com/pod-product-compliance
Lightning Source LLC
Chambersburg PA
CBHW071138130626

46553CB00004B/1430